GOD'S ACRE

GOD'S ACRE

*The flowers and
animals of the parish churchyard*

Francesca Greenoak

Illustrations by
Clare Roberts

Foreword by
Richard Mabey

ORBIS · LONDON

Published in Great Britain by
Orbis Publishing Limited, London 1985

ISBN: 0-85613-800-2

Produced by WI Books Ltd., 39 Eccleston Street, London SW1W 9N.
Managing editor: Sue Parish
Designer: David Goodman
Editors: Flax Green Associates
Filmsetting: Tradespools Limited, Frome, Somerset
Colour reproduction: Preager Blackmore Limited, Eastbourne, Sussex
Printed and bound in the Netherlands by: Royal Smeets Offset bv, Weert

Yet their continued existence cannot be taken for granted. Our growing concern for them is comparatively new, and it is only slowly establishing its importance against other claims on the worldly territory of the Church. At present, churchyards are regarded principally as resting places for the dead, where a respectful, sombre tidiness, clipped of the excesses of nature, ought to prevail. That is an understandable feeling, but in the light of our growing sense of the interdependence of all life, a more hospitable attitude towards the rest of natural creation might perhaps be an apter Christian response.

As it happens, ideas for reconciling these different views are flourishing. Many involve the resumption of practices which were common when churchyards were partly looked on as the church's 'outside room' and expected to play their part in the intricate community affairs of the parish. I treasure a glimpse a few years ago of a revival of the whole cycle of cloth-making. It was at Worstead in Norfolk, birthplace of one of England's most famous fabrics. Sheep grazed in the churchyard, spinning wheels and looms were at work in the aisles, and the finished cloth was used for renewing the hassocks.

I hope the eloquent arguments in this book will hasten this process of reconciliation, for the challenge of ensuring that churchyards serve the diverse needs of a whole community – and that includes the needs of its wild creatures – is a microcosm of the environmental challenges that face us all. And it is a challenge, moreover, in which the spiritual significance of nature is for once given its rightful place.

RICHARD MABEY

The church of St Mary and St Michael, in Great Urswick, Cumbria, with its fine Scots pine.

AUTHOR'S NOTE AND ACKNOWLEDGEMENTS

A NEW ROLE FOR CHURCHYARDS HAS emerged over the last decade – that of nature conservation. There are more than twenty thousand churchyards set around churches and chapels of various denominations in England and Wales. Church and chapel yards vary in size from a pocket handkerchief lawn to several acres, but it has been calculated that the average extent works out, approximately, at about an acre. Taken altogether this represents a sizeable area of land which has survived untouched by either urban development or intensive agriculture, and as such, churchyards have assumed an importance not only for the people of the parish but for its wildlife also. This book looks at the natural history of churchyards and how it can be supported, in the context of their social and community functions.

Much of the research for this book originated with the Women's Institute, whose members noted plants, animals, boundaries, habitats of various kinds, and churchyard ceremonies all over England and Wales during the course of no less than fourteen hundred individual churchyard surveys. Similarly, a number of other organizations – the Botanical Society of the British Isles, the Lichen Society, the county Bat Groups, the British Butterfly Conservation Society, the British Trust for Ornithology – have focused their attention on churchyards and carried out survey work of their own. I have drawn on the work of these specialist groups, generously made available to me to complement my own personal observations.

The idea for this book was not my own, but was originated several years ago by the late John Talbot White in collaboration with Sue Parish (now Manager of WI Books); I am very grateful to Sue for her responsiveness and encouragement during a very full year of travelling, research and writing, in which she made every effort to lighten the load for me. When she brought me into the project, she had already organized the extensive churchyard survey made through the Women's Institute's network of volunteers.

It was only after the sad death of John White in 1983 that I was asked whether I would look at the survey with a view to writing the book. The paragraph which begins my book would, if things had been different, have been the opening to his.

In the writing of this book, I have been advised, criticised and helped most generously by many people involved in different ways with churchyards. My deepest thanks to Arthur Chater, Botanical Recorder for Cardiganshire, who has surveyed all hundred and one churchyards in that region, for his guidance and encouragement and for setting such a high standard of clear-headedness and style in his own work. As one of my dearest friends, Richard Mabey was by far the most ruthless in shaking many misconceptions and structural and stylistic weaknesses out of my first draft.

Mary Briggs of the Botanical Society of the British Isles not only introduced me to those people in the forefront of churchyard research but kept me supplied tirelessly with notes and observations on the subject I am indebted to Phil Richardson for introducing me to bat-watching in churchyards and to Jack Laundon for his help with the lichens. My thanks go also to David Glue of the British Trust for Ornithology for his observations on churchyard birds. I am grateful to all of these for corrections and comments on various drafts of the book, and especially to Philip Oswald of the Nature Conservancy Council who read and corrected the revised typescript. Credit must be given also to Veronica Watkins who so quickly and efficiently turned indecipherable pages into fair copy.

I am a devoted admirer of Francis Simpson's *Flora of Suffolk* and it was a great pleasure to discuss with him his researches in churchyards which have extended over many years. I was almost sidetracked for good into the fascinations of churchyard archaeology by acquaintance with Dr Warwick Rodwell, who kindly sent me proofs of his book *Our Christian Heritage* and directed me to the CBA research report on churches and churchyards.

I shall remember this period, in which I visited over two hundred churchyards, with particular affection, especially those occasions when I was initiated by other churchyard devotees into knowledge of plants and animals new to me. I am grateful to Dr Francis Rose for the crash course in lichen identification in a beautiful Hampshire churchyard, to Dr Chris Hitch for perambulating Leiston churchyard in Suffolk with me on a similar quest, and to Joy Fildes who sought out several new species on my home ground at Wigginton. I recall with great pleasure a foray into Cambridgeshire churchyards with the ex-warden and Director of Studies at Flatford Field Centre, F.J. Bingley MBE, who led some pioneer churchyard survey work. Another memorable occasion was the July day spent with Dr

Soldier beetles congregating and mating on flowerheads in July in the grounds of the redundant church, at Corpusty, Norfolk. (Life size).

Frank Perring of the Royal Society for Nature Conservation, Angela Walker of the Northamptonshire Trust for Nature Conservation and the County Recorder for Botany, Mrs Gill Gent, when they judged the county churchyard competition. I am always glad to visit Ted Ellis, who is, on this subject as on so many others, enthusiastic and widely knowledgeable, and who readily supplied me with a list of topical and literary references.

There were many others who enriched my understanding of the subject through conversation and correspondence. Among these were George Barker, author of the booklet *Wildlife Conservation in the Care of Churches and Churchyards* published in 1972, an early landmark in churchyard conservation; Rev Canon Henry Stapleton, whose edition of the *Churchyard Handbook* was an important milestone; Eva Crackles who investigated herb-planting in churchyards; Dr Alan Leslie who made a study of the goldilocks buttercup with reference to churchyard populations; and Alison Rutherford who has cast new light on ivies. I received generous help from many County Recorders for botany, and both clergymen and laypeople wrote to me about churchyard customs and traditions. I am sorry there was too much correspondence to acknowledge everyone here individually. For helpful guidance in the reference library of the Council for the Care of Churches I am grateful to the librarian David Williams and to the assistant librarian Janet Seeley.

Working alongside Clare Roberts has been both a pleasure and an inspiration. She herself would like to thank Rosemary, Bryan and Simon Roberts for their invaluable help and encouragement. On behalf of Sue Parish, I would like to mention the work of Joy Potter and Richard Firdon on the WI questionnaires and to thank them. Thanks are due also to John Murray for John Betjeman's 'Sunday Afternoon Service in St Enodoc Church, Cornwall' and 'Wantage Bells' collected in *Church Poems*, first published in 1981 and to Oxford University Press for 'Manchán's Wish' from *Early Irish Lyrics*, translated by Gerard Murphy (1956).

I should not have been able to write this book without the help and support of my husband John who took on even more than usual of the domestic organization and gave up all his holidays to care for the children while I was away or in seclusion at my desk. A word too for Barbara and Ronald Kilpatrick who were always there to help when needed and for Alice and Howarth who accompanied me on many churchyard visits.

HISTORY
and
HERITAGE

The churchyard, God's acre, is one of the most enduring features of the landscape. Together with the church it forms the physical as well as the spiritual centre of the community. It is the most sacred and usually the most ancient enclosure in the parish. Some churchyards may be even older than the church itself, having their roots in pre-Christian ceremony. The memorials, public and private, are a tangible link between the inhabitants today and their forebears. The churchyard is the centre of communal worship and celebration, the site of the most important occasions of life, baptism, marriage and burial.

John Talbot White

THERE IS SOMETHING WHICH DRAWS PEOPLE, non-churchgoers as well as religious folk, to churchyards. They have a quality that is quite out of the ordinary. A kind of peace exists within them, whether they are set in wild isolation or in the centre of a town or village. Many churchyards are places which have been held sacred for hundreds, sometimes thousands of years, and I do not think it fanciful to believe that outdoor places quite as much as buildings can convey a sense of antiquity and sanctity.

The sense that a churchyard may have an existence that is beyond time and the everyday world is sometimes very strong. The writing of this book began at such a place. Winter evening was beginning to close in as I drove along the causeway between wide ploughed fields to the church of Tilbury-juxta-Clare in Essex. The little circular churchyard was like a bushy island, and the setting sun outlined the shapes of the medieval church and the tall limes of the boundary hedge with their dark nests of mistletoe.

The flora bore testimony to long, continuous care. At the entrance, there was a glossy, dark green mass of periwinkle, 'joy of the ground', the herb which 'hath an excellent value to stench bleeding at the nose in Christians if it be made into a garland and hung about the neck'. There were clumps of gladdon, which is often found in churchyards, the swordlike leaves a rich evergreen, the pods opened to reveal neat lines of

The flowers of stinking hellebore attract bees on a cool March day. (Life size).

Stinking hellebore in bud, in late January at St Margaret's, Tilbury-juxta-Clare, Essex.

14

brilliant orange seeds. Beside a gravestone near the south porch grew stinking hellebore, with strange, pale green flowers edged in purple. It is native to Essex, but has been planted, bird-sown or seeded itself in churchyards there and in neighbouring counties. Near the hellebore, tall briars arched around the gravestones. By the boundary hedge snowdrops were just beginning to appear, the flowerheads like white-tipped spears, preparing to open in February as the flower of Candlemas. The first small leaves of primroses and cowslips were emerging in the grass on and around the graves, and mallows had started into growth beneath the elegant curves of the ivy, both sheltered by the wall of the church tower.

Startled wrens flew out of the masonry and into thick clumps of hazel as I passed by. There was hazel also, together with field maple and blackthorn, in the hedge which topped the low bank of the boundary enclosing the church. Two century-old limes flanked the entrance to the churchyard. Their rough, ivy-covered trunks bristled with an abundant growth of suckers from the base, and mistletoe hung high in the branches. In the failing light, lichens made soft shapes of grey and orange-brown on the gravestones. I could hear ducks quacking in the distance and, when I turned to leave, a large kestrel, her long, sharp-edged wings curved back for landing, was briefly silhouetted against the silky winter sky before vanishing into the shadow of the tower.

There are churchyards as rich as this to be found all over the British Isles. They provide almost every kind of habitat from seashore and rocky coast to chalk grassland, heath and deep woodland. Once, they simply reflected the abundant wildlife in the countryside around them. Nowadays they are all too often little islands of riches set in land so intensively used for agriculture, urban development or afforestation that its traditional fauna and flora have been driven out. In the face of increasing pressure on the chalk grasslands, it is perhaps significant that the three plants which go by the vernacular name of 'sanctuary' in some counties — centaury, yellow-wort and red bartsia — all flowers of the chalk, have found refuge in churchyards.

In some parts of Britain, the name for the churchyard itself was 'sanctuary', and until the sixteenth century any fugitive (unless charged with sacrilege or treason) could claim sanctuary on entering its consecrated ground. Nowadays it is wildlife, rather than human-kind, that needs

Ivy climbing the church wall of St Margaret's, Tilbury-juxta-Clare, Essex.

The church at St Margaret's,
Tilbury-juxta-Clare, Essex,
from the east.

the refuge of the churchyard. Inside these sheltered confines
live flowering plants (wild, naturalized and cultivated), lichens
and fungi, and a wide range of animal life: gravestone invertebrates less
than a millimetre long, large insects such as dor beetles; glow-worms;
butterflies, moths and bees; frogs, toads, snakes, lizards and slow-worms;
birds of many kinds; a host of small mammals such as moles, shrews and
voles; bats, and even some larger mammals, hares and rabbits, stoats and
weasels, foxes and badgers.

Although my principal concern was natural history, I could not
help but be struck during the course of my travels by the human activity in
churchyards. Whether there was a footpath across the churchyard or not,
there were often people walking there. On even the most bitter of winter
days, there might be someone tending a grave, clipping a hedge or
mowing. In a chapelyard at Capel Rhiwbws, Dyfed, people in adjoining
houses draped their washing over the gravestones to dry. Occasionally, a
group of children melted into the boundary hedge or a verger came to pin
something up in the porch. The church porch is a good
barometer of the place of church and churchyard in parish
life. Apart from the official diocesan and electoral notices,
there are announcements of events in the church and parish,
rotas for flower arranging, sometimes a brief history of
the church. At St Peter's, Mildenhall, in Suffolk there is a
notice explaining the association between the village name and
the plant 'meld', now usually called fat hen, which is believed
to have grown locally since neolithic times.

The churchyard has a special meaning for the people
of a parish — for those who go to church, walk in procession on
Palm Sunday, sing carols at Christmas and who are christened,
married and eventually buried there. It also means a great
deal to others who do none of these things, but who

Welsh poppies (leaves illustrated above) thriving in the churchyard at St Margaret's, Binsey, in Oxfordshire, in July. They are not native this far east, but naturalize readily from grave plantings or nearby gardens.

simply care about the place where they live. It has always been the local people who look after the churchyard, doing maintenance work such as weeding, and minor repairs. By the seventeenth century it had become the practice in some places for churchwardens to make local landowners responsible for keeping the churchyard boundary walls and fences in good repair. At Cowfold in Sussex the fence was maintained by eighty-one parishioners — their initials can be found carved into some of the palings — and at Chiddingley in the same county fifty-six parishioners looked after varying stretches of fencing, allocated according to their means. Churchwardens' accounts, as far back as medieval times, show that, even then, people were concerned about the way the churchyard was kept, and they would complain and, as a final resort, even take legal action if they thought it was being misused.

Generally speaking, the presence of wild flora and fauna in the churchyard interferes little or not at all with human requirements, although in recent years new techniques of mowing and weed control have started to be applied in churchyards, and conflict has begun to arise. The old-fashioned churchyards are the most hospitable to wildlife and, in truth, to many of their human visitors too.

It is no paradox that churchyards support a thriving fauna and flora. In Christian tradition, as well as in the natural world, there is always life in the midst of death, and churchyards are not morbid places. Benefactors, private and public, often give benches to the churchyard and it is pleasant to sit among the flowers and the warm lichen colours of the gravestones on a sunny day. There, one can observe a friendly interaction between people and nature. The chiming of bells or the muffled sounds of the organ mingle with birdsong and the busy sound of insects or the squeak of a shrew. Although many churchyards provide a home for plants and animals which are regionally and sometimes nationally rare, it would be a shame if they were regarded simply as nature reserves; they are more than that.

St John the Baptist, in Ysbyty Cynfyn, Dyfed.

In these consecrated surroundings it is both possible and desirable for civilization and wildlife to exist in harmony. The churchyard may be a quiet place for reflection, a burial ground and a home and shelter for a wide range of animals and plants. Many of the problems with maintenance experienced by incumbents arise because they try to make the churchyard over-tidy. The flowery meadow of cowslips, fritillaries, orchids and other flowers beloved of people in medieval times, was both beautiful and fertile, and this is a better model for the churchyard than a bowling green. At the other extreme, the ground may be so neglected that coarse, rank vegetation smothers the lichens and small flowers and obscures the graves. The ideal of minimal and judicious management can benefit both the vegetation and the creatures that live in it, so that those who enter the churchyard, whether visitor, churchgoer or mourner, can feel comfortable. It is all the more important nowadays, when so many churches' doors are kept locked except during services, for the churchyard to be a pleasant and meditative place.

Places full of wild flowers and birds, real and miraculous, are associated with the early Christian Church, and the history of the first British saints is touched with details and attitudes towards nature that we associate with earlier religions. According to legend, St Nonna, mother of the patron saint of Wales, finding herself caught in a violent storm, took shelter within a circle of stones. There she found blue sky, sunshine and the song of birds, while the storm continued to rage outside. Soon afterwards, she bore her son, St David, and the place within the stones (believed to have been a stone circle dedicated to the earth and its plenty), at Llannon in Dyfed, became a Christian chapel and chapelyard.

There were many saints who sought places in remote country to live and pray, and chose for company birds and animals rather than men. Almost every representation of St Cuthbert portrays his love for the wildlife of the Farne Islands, and it took the king and some of the most devout men of the northern kingdom to persuade him to exchange his hermit cell in the wilderness for a bishopric. In the account written by the Venerable Bede, Cuthbert wept when they 'eventually drew him from his beloved retreat' and pined so greatly that he returned after two years. St Guthlac, another seventh-century saint, gave up wealth and title for a life of Christian humility and self-denial. He chose for his home the wildest and most

It is still widely held that these two upright stones (and three others) built into the church wall of St John the Baptist, at Ysbyty Cynfyn, Dyfed, were once part of a pre-Christian stone circle – although modern scholars have cast doubts on the subject.

isolated place he could find, a small island in the fens. Ancient spirits
haunted him there, not surprisingly, since it appears to have been the sacred
place of an earlier people:

> There was on the island a certain great burial ground built over the earth
> . . . On one side of the burial mound there was dug a great well of water.
> Over this the blessed Guthlac built himself a house.

This remote retreat became Crowland Abbey, the north part of which is
now a parish church. It is hard to believe that it was once an island. Even
the strange triangular bridge nearby in the town, built in the fourteenth
century to span two streams, now stretches over dry land. In fact, there is
hardly any of the original wetland habitat left in Lincolnshire, and none of
the wilderness St Guthlac inhabited, though there is wildness in the scream
of the swifts as they sweep through the Norman arch of the ruined Abbey
just above the place where the saint's cell used to be. There is still a feeling

*A magnificent yew dominates the
churchyard of St Nicholas, Asthall,
Oxfordshire.*

for plants in the parish, tamed perhaps but still strong, for the Crowland Abbey flower festival has become famous.

      The fact that St Guthlac's chosen home at Crowland lay over a site previously venerated by an earlier people is by no means exceptional. There are many examples of churches and chapels built on or close to the holy places of older religions. In 1529, Thomas More gave expression to what seems to have been a long-held tradition of continuity of worship, writing that 'it is clear that God wishes to be worshipped in particular places'. Pope Gregory the Great certainly believed so, and in a letter to Abbot Melitus who was shortly to join St Augustine in England, observed that people would 'continue to frequent the same sacred places' even if the altar there was dedicated to a new god. When Gregory also recommended that the ancient sites and temples of the Britons be appropriated rather than destroyed, he seems to have been acknowledging a tolerance which was already operating. Archaeological evidence, like some folk legends, suggests that the transition from earlier forms of worship, Roman or

A jackdaws' nest with its tenants in the square church tower of St Brynach, Nevern, Dyfed.

British, to Christianity was in many cases peaceful, though there were notable outbreaks of persecution. Work on the temple of Mithras in Queen Victoria Street in London has shown that the building was methodically turned to Christian use after a ceremonial burial of the trappings of the old gods. At Lullingstone in Kent, the private pagan shrine of the villa was converted for Christian worship in about AD 350, and other instances of conversion of this kind occurred in Roman Britain. Evidence from that period found in the city of Bath suggests that a supplicant might invoke the Christian and a pagan god in a single entreaty.

Archaeological excavation has traced the continuity of use of some churchyards back to prehistory. In the case of Crowland, the site was an ancient burial mound; other churchyards are set on early places of worship, burial grounds or within prehistoric hilltop enclosures. At Winwick in Cheshire, a church and churchyard lie over a Bronze Age barrow, and burial urns indicating the presence of barrows of the same period have been found in several other churchyards. An Iron Age burial was discovered in St Martin's churchyard at Wharram Percy in North Yorkshire. Among the most striking examples of churches which are set within ancient earthworks are St Mary's at Breedon-on-the-Hill, in Leicestershire, where the original monastery was founded inside an Iron Age hill fort, and the ruined church at Knowlton in Dorset, which stands dramatically at the centre of a Bronze Age henge monument.

Little is known of the religions which preceded Christianity in Britain but it is generally accepted that the Celtic peoples venerated places of exceptional natural beauty, such as hilltops, groves of trees, springs and rivers. It could be argued that churches and churchyards inherited not only the physical sites but a tradition of seeking out places of special beauty and atmosphere.

Celtic poetry is imbued with this strong respect for the natural world. Indeed, for guidance on the sensitive conservation of holy ground we might look to the Celtic ideal in which love of God is expressed in love of nature. This idea is epitomized in a tenth-century poem of unknown authorship, written about the saint, Manchán of Liath, in southern Ireland, three centuries earlier.

Manchán's Wish

I wish, O son of the living God, eternal ancient King, for a hidden little hut in the wilderness that it might be my dwelling,

All-grey shallow water beside it, a clear pool to wash away sins through the grace of the Holy Spirit,

A beautiful wood close by, surrounding it on every side, for the nurture of many-voiced birds, for shelter to hide them,

A southern aspect for warmth, a little stream across its glebe, choice land of abundant bounty which would be good for every plant,

A few young men of sense, we shall tell their number, humble and obedient to pray the King:

Four threes, three fours, (to suit every need), two sixes in the church, both north and south;

Six couples in addition to myself ever praying to the King who makes the sun shine;

A lovely church decked with linen, a dwelling for God from heaven, bright lights, then, above the pure white scriptures,

One house to go to for tending the body, without meditation of evil.

This is the husbandry which I would undertake and openly choose genuine fragrant leeks, hens, speckled salmon, bees, –

Raiment and food enough for me from the King whose fame is fair, to be seated for a time, and to pray to God in some place.

[*translation: Gerard Murphy*]

The Great Celtic Cross in St Brynach's churchyard, Nevern, Dyfed, which dates from the tenth or eleventh century. Legend says that on April 7 (the patron's day) every year, a cuckoo perches on the cross.

There are no clear facts about how early churchyards were established. Ecclesiastical authorities seem to have advocated burial of Christians within the precincts of the church from at least the time of Gregory the Great, who believed that churchgoers who passed by graves on their way into church would then remember the dead in their prayers. The parish system (or something approximating very closely to it) was established in England and Wales as early as the tenth century, and it was the ordinary Christians of the parish who were buried in the churchyards. Clergy and important personages were interred in the church itself.

Saxon landowners were encouraged to build churches on their land and complied to such an extent that almost certainly most English churches in rural areas came into existence during the late Saxon period. In the latter half of the tenth century, there was also inducement to freehold landowners to establish churchyards, for if a church was given a burial ground, it became entitled to a third of the tithes, which were otherwise due to the minster which administered the district. It is interesting to note that as the Church became increasingly powerful and its ownership of land more extensive, the spirit of this law was reversed. Henry III's Statutes of Mortmain, dating from 1279, forbade individuals to give land to the Church, though this law seems not always to have been obeyed. By the reign of George III it was again legal to donate land to the Church; up to five acres could be given for the provision of a churchyard, glebe or residence for the incumbent.

Although the Welsh king Hywel Dda prescribed an area of one acre in 943, churchyards appear always to have differed widely in shape and size. The name 'God's Acre' is Teutonic in origin and seems not to have been mentioned in England until references in the early seventeenth century specifically to German churchyards. The German *Gottesacker* and Dutch *Godsakker* were terms not primarily concerned with churchyard area. The meaning was more accurately 'God's seed field' in which the bodies of the faithful – the 'seed' – are the potential harvest of the Resurrection. The basis of this idea seems to be the evocative words of St Paul's First Epistle to the Corinthians (chapter 15):

Oxford ragwort on the churchyard wall of St Peter-in-the-East, Oxford, seen in mid-July. (The Church is now used as the library of St Edmund Hall).

How are the dead raised? . . .

There is one glory of the sun, and another
glory of the moon, and another glory of the
stars: for one star differeth from another
star in glory.

So also is the resurrection of the dead. It is
sown in corruption; it is raised in incorruption.

It is sown in dishonour; it is raised in
glory: it is sown in weakness; it is
raised in power:

It is sown a natural body; it is raised
a spiritual body.

One can only guess at what the early churchyards looked like and what
plant life they supported. It is almost certain that most of them were
enclosed. The 'yard' of churchyard derives, like the word 'garden' and
'garth' (still used to refer to churchyards in Scotland and the north of
England) from the Old English word *geard*, which means an enclosed space.
It is thought that the cemeteries of monastic foundations were the model for
parish churchyards, and monasteries generally had several kinds of yard in
which plants were grown.

One of the earliest depictions of monastery building and land
configuration is the eighth-century plan of St Gall. This is not the actual
plan for the St Gall foundation, a Benedictine house near Lake Constance,
but is thought to be a theoretical representation of ideas current at the time.
In the grounds are a cloister garden, a physic garden and a kitchen garden.
The cemetery, enclosed by walls and hedges, contains fruit trees and
shrubs, but no other plants.

In addition to their other garden-enclosures, abbeys and
monasteries had one or more highly cultivated gardens under the care of the
sacristan. These '*gardini Sacristi*' provided most of the very large quantity of
flowers and greenery required to decorate the church and to make garlands

*Common centaury, the
sanctuary flower, in bloom
in a Suffolk churchyard in
June. (Life size).*

27

or floral wreaths for the clergy on feast days and major religious festivals. Larger churches and well-endowed chapels possessed similar gardens, which remained separate from the churchyard proper. Henry VI bequeathed land for such a garden to the chapel of Eton College 'for to sett in certain trees and flowers, behovable and convenient for the service of the same church'. Churchwardens' accounts list some of the plants which were used, such as box and willow-palm on Palm Sunday, garlands of roses and woodruff for Corpus Christi, roses on St Martin's Day, birch at Midsummer, and holly and ivy at Christmas.

Church decoration became illegal after the Reformation and, although there is considerable evidence that the new plain orthodoxy of service was often ignored (people do not lightly give up their accustomed modes of worship), it was then impossible to keep up elaborate and costly church gardens. Some were sold or fell into dereliction; others, particularly those adjacent to the churchyard, may have been absorbed. Poorer churches and small ones which would not have boasted gardens must have carried on much as usual, probably growing a small variety of flowers within the churchyard. The tended beds of churchyards may possibly be distantly related to those old church gardens.

In the past, the traditional practice of maintaining the churchyard in much the same way as a meadow, by grazing or infrequent mowing, kept the plants and animals in healthy community. However, relatively few people now know or can remember the beauty and fertility of an ancient meadow. Increasingly, the model for a churchyard is that of a suburban garden, scrupulously neat and close-mown. It is both difficult to keep up in a large area like a churchyard and damaging to the wildlife community. The wide range of plants and the animals which depend on them cannot survive in such a churchyard.

We know from a variety of sources that churchyards in the past suffered mismanagement. Unsuitable animals such as pigs, cattle or horses were kept in some; others were overgrazed and the flora depleted, while yet others were left to become impenetrable wildernesses. The state of the churchyard became a perennial cause for complaint among parishioners. Sometimes crops were grown in the churchyard. It is said that an eighteenth-century rector was rebuked by his archdeacon for growing turnips in the churchyard. He hoped to see no such thing when he came

A traditional stone stile built into the wall gives entry to the churchyard, St Mary and St Michael, Great Urswick, Cumbria.

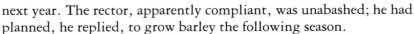

next year. The rector, apparently compliant, was unabashed; he had planned, he replied, to grow barley the following season.

Up until the last few decades, a churchyard which had been ill-treated could recover itself. Grasses and wild flowers would grow again, replenished by seed from the meadows and waysides surrounding the churchyard. This is no longer the case; in fact, in some counties the churchyard is the last reserve for wildlife in a parish. A churchyard may have its origins in prehistory, but its importance as a place for quiet reflection and the appreciation of the beauty and diversity of nature may extend far into the future.

It is impossible to look at churchyards today without acknowledging the debt to the past. What makes a churchyard's small compass so interesting in terms of its fauna and flora is largely the diversity of habitat there. This is not a condition brought about by natural causes. The items of which a naturalist takes special account in a churchyard – the boundary walls and hedges, the mature trees, the quality of the grassy spaces, the memorials – have not arrived there accidentally: they are the result of a long interaction between human and natural history.

It is nearly always easy to locate a churchyard without difficulty; the familiar tower or spire signals its presence to us now, just as it has to people since medieval times. The bird species which inhabit these lofty places seem to be remarkably similar, too. From the early sixteenth century, there are scattered mentions in churchwardens' accounts from all over the country of jackdaws, owls, pigeons and starlings. Then as now, birds seem to have been tolerated in the churchyard and church fabric, but not inside the church. Measures taken against birds were occasionally violent, but more often they simply entailed the preventative stopping-up of crevices, holes and gaps in walls and roofs. At Bradeston in Norfolk, the parishioners seem to have made an equivalent in net of the modern 'bird-door', for their accounts list a payment for 'Twynne for ye nette at ye church dore'.

Yews are the tree species most associated with churchyards and it can be convincingly argued that certain churchyard yews may be the oldest living things in Britain. However, many other tree species are associated

Goldfinches eating the seeds of creeping thistle in a Gloucestershire churchyard.

with churchyards. There is a most interesting reference to the churchyard elms of St Edmund, Sarum, which must have been mature trees in 1644, since the accounts note that six of them were felled and the rest lopped. The wood was sold to help provide the cost of repairs to the church and its south windows. It is evident that new elms were planted, for in 1650–51 there was a payment for watering 'the young trees' during the summer; they did not all thrive, for there was a resolution in the winter of 1693 to plant 'Elm trees in the room of those that are dead, and as many more as the C.W. [churchwardens] shall think convenient', whereupon sixteen more elms and three sycamores were supplied, planted and tended by a certain 'William Baker gardener'.

Avenues of fastigiate yews such as this one leading to the town church of St Giles, Oxford, are a common sight in churchyards. Sadly, people seem to have given up planting the traditional common yew and have turned to this stumpy, upswept form.

31

It seems likely, however, that before the eighteenth century, many, if not most, of the churchyard trees were brought in as young saplings from local woodland, rather than purchased. This seems to have happened on the borders of West Suffolk in the late seventeenth and early eighteenth centuries. In the churchyards of Groton and Lindsey and by the lane to Great Waldringfield church, all of which are in the vicinity of the ancient limewoods of this region, the woodland specialist, Dr Oliver Rackham, has identified old lime trees of indigenous genotypes. Almost certainly in these parishes, the churchwardens of old made their choice from the most plentiful and striking trees in the wild: the small-leaved lime, a species that is dense and shapely in maturity, burred and bristly in venerable old age.

There is much still to be uncovered about the history of tree-planting in churchyards. From the evidence that we have, the eighteenth century seems to have been a period of considerable enterprise in churchyards, as it was in parkland and great gardens, and the nineteenth century saw not only nationwide work on the 'restoration' of church fabric but also extensive planting. The archaeologist Dr Warwick Rodwell has

outlined a convincing theory that the churchyard elms at Rivenhall in Essex were planted by the landscape gardener, Humphrey Repton, when he was landscaping Rivenhall Park in 1791. While remodelling the church in 1838–39, Repton's son added a formal arrangement of yews, cedars, cypresses and holm oaks. Most of the eighteenth-century elm planting has been wiped out by Dutch elm disease, leaving skeletons or (as at Kedington, Suffolk) great gaps along the boundaries. The healthy elms I saw in West Yorkshire were a sad reminder of how beautiful they had once been elsewhere.

Cedars were a very popular churchyard tree throughout the nineteenth century. In a revealing series of illustrations hanging in the church of St George at Saham Toney in Norfolk, you can see that in 1779 there was a scrupulously neat churchyard with no trees. An illustration dating from 1820 shows a tomb beside an elm, and the latest, dated 1893, has several new trees – cedars, yews and some other conifers. Several of these trees, including the cedars and yews, are still to be seen in the churchyard. At Much Dewchurch, a few miles south of Hereford, there is a large stump around and on which grow spreading honeysuckle, ivy-leaved toadflax, and a few failing roses. I was told that it was a larch stump, and it was only by chance that I discovered that this old tree had in fact been another of the old cedars, felled because they were past their prime, or casting too much shade. The verger kindly showed me round the church, where I happened to see the church banner, which has embroidered on it in silk a beautiful and accurate view of the church and churchyard showing the unmistakable spreading branches of a Lebanon cedar in the place of the old stump.

The big trees of the churchyard are usually yew, lime, beech and horse chestnut, sometimes planted in avenues from the lych-gate to the south porch, or ranged on the boundary to provide a leafy shelterbelt. Large trees were often planted in groups of twelve to represent the apostles. At Acton in Suffolk the lane sloping up to the church is flanked on either side by an impressive avenue of no less than forty-three limes, believed to be about a hundred years old and said to have been planted during the 1885 restoration scheme. Along the path to the church at East Tuddenham in Norfolk, twenty common lime trees, probably planted in about 1810, at the time when the lych-gate was erected, form a shady avenue in striking contrast to the open brightness of the churchyard.

A pair of parent wrens, seen at St John the Baptist, Fifield, Oxfordshire, in late July.

This living lych-gate of yew at St Margaret's, Warnham in Sussex, is over a hundred years old. Twenty years ago, it was even larger, but because it overhung the pavement, it was clipped back by the vicar to its present shape.

*Scanty elderberries in a churchyard
hedge in Dorset, at the beginning of
October. The missing ones have
almost certainly been eaten by birds,
who take full advantage of this early
autumn feast. (Life size).*

The plantings of the last two hundred years have included a number of exotic conifers. Besides cedars, Wellingtonia and even monkey puzzles were popular with the Victorians. Today the choice is more likely to include the ubiquitous Lawson's cypress, which even an admirer of conifers, Alan Mitchell, calls 'the commonest and most gloomy conifer throughout these islands'. It is exceedingly tough and produces an astounding variety of different forms, all equally robust. The presence of these and other conifers provide breeding places for little birds and are particularly important for coal tits and goldcrests.

It is generally agreed that, by the Middle Ages, most churchyards were enclosed by a definite wall, hedge or bank. Archaeological work has shown that these boundaries often changed shape over the years, but nevertheless many of the hedges and walls surrounding churchyards are of great age. Ancient hedges usually contain a large number of species. Field maple, holly, crab apple, rose, elder and hazel are often found, together with the more conventional hawthorn and blackthorn. Some hedgerow planting has a local distribution, such as the cherry plum in north-west Hertfordshire or the Duke of Argyll's tea plant in Suffolk. Oak, ash, beech and elm are among the larger species that are also found in hedges, mainly clipped into the hedge, but occasionally left to grow to maturity. Large trees are most often to be found at the main entrance to the churchyard, on either side of the gate.

Mature trees of churchyard and hedge provide effective shelter for birds, mammals and insects, particularly in areas where woods and hedges are otherwise scarce. They are of especial benefit to birds which may feed, roost and nest in them. In Edlesborough churchyard in Buckinghamshire, I counted twenty nests in the trees and shrubs. Churches in prominent positions provide navigational landmarks and stopping places for some species (spotted flycatchers, for instance) on migration. By contrast, there are butterflies, some of the hairstreaks for example, which depend on a single tree species and which may live out their entire life cycle in and around one large churchyard tree.

The fragrant pink-white beauty of crab apple blossom graces a churchyard boundary hedge at Snead, Powys, in mid-May. (Life size).

The other main type of boundary, the churchyard wall, also repays thorough investigation both as a historical artefact and for its natural history. It is not unusual for stone walls to contain carved blocks from earlier buildings, which can sometimes be dated back as far as Roman times. At Heysham in Lancashire, a complete Anglo-Saxon doorway from the church has been rebuilt into the wall.

Old stone churchyard walls are especially important for wildlife in areas where there is little or no local stone. In Suffolk and Cambridgeshire most of the county records for certain ferns refer to specimens growing on church and churchyard walls. Some of these fern observations have a long history. Black spleenwort, which is a common plant in fern-rich counties but rare in Cambridgeshire, was seen on the walls of Ditton and Hildersham by the eminent naturalist, John Ray, and recorded in the Second Appendix to his *Cambridge Catalogue* published in 1685. Another clergyman-botanist, Richard Relhan, also recorded it at these two churches in 1785. In Babington's *Flora of Cambridgeshire*, which was published in 1860 at the height of a period of intense enthusiasm for ferns, nearly all of an increased number of references to black spleenwort are from church and churchyard sites. Twentieth-century observers report that it seems no longer to grow in the two original sites, but have discovered three other church locations for it in Cambridgeshire.

There is usually a thriving assembly of flowering plants on churchyard walls, of which some are of historical note. The 'wild' yellow wallflower, possibly introduced with imported Caen stone in Norman times, survives mainly on church and castle walls and church towers. The plants growing on the abbey ruins at Bury St Edmunds appear to be identical to the wild species. One of only a handful of sites for the now-extinct umbellate chickweed was within Norwich cathedral precincts, while the rare spotted hawkweed, originally observed at Norwich, is now found on the walls of some churches in the surrounding countryside. A more common plant of church grounds is the Oxford ragwort, which spread from the botanical garden to a college wall and thence, in the nineteenth century, along railway lines throughout the country to colonize waste places, town gardens, and churchyard and other walls. The process of colonization continues: I have seen both pink and purple varieties of aubrieta, presumably escaped from neighbouring

A blackcap's nest in brambles by the churchyard hedge of St Mary's at Glemsfold in Suffolk.

St MARGARETS WELL

S. MARGARETÆ FONTEM
RECIBVS S. FRIDESWIDÆ VT FERTVR CONCES
INQVINATVM DV OBRVTVMQVE
IN VSVM REVOCAVIT
T J. PROVT ÆD·XTI ALVMNVS VICARIVS
A.S. MDCCCLXXIV

gardens, spilling over churchyard walls. It is a pretty, if to some eyes rather suburban, sight, and welcome to brimstone butterflies which feed enthusiastically on the flowers.

Churchyard memorials are interesting territory for the naturalist as well as the historian. Self-sown trees often grow from tombs and grave-beds. At Selborne in Hampshire, such growth is turned to advantage. Sycamores emerging from all sides of the top slab of a chest tomb form a leafy screen, which is apparently pruned back to a discreet bushy rectangle each winter. In many churchyards, neat little grave plantings of box have

The holy well at St Margaret's, Binsey, Oxfordshire, which provided Saint Frideswide and her followers with fresh water. It is believed to have curative powers for eye ailments. The area around the well provides a damp habitat for ferns such as the hartstongue and polypody. Above it, Solomon's seal mingles with the foliage of Japanese anemone.

grown into great billowing bushes which completely engulf the stones, providing year-round shelter for birds and other animals. In the small and secluded churchyard at Strethall in Essex, a haven for birds. I stood by a tall box tree and watched a woodpigeon on her nest in July, incubating yet another pair of eggs when the youngsters of most other species were already fledged and flying.

Churchyard memorial stone is, above all, a habitat for those insubstantial but beautiful and long-lived plants: the lichens. Some country churchyards support over a hundred different species, which glow orange, buttercup yellow, blue-green and grey against the stone. There are good historical, conservationist and scientific reasons for keeping churchyard gravestones in place. The lichens which grow on gravestones are attractive to look at, frequently of regional interest and sometimes rare. If the stones are moved, the lichens are almost invariably destroyed. Because they are extremely sensitive to pollution, lichens have been used in recent years to monitor levels of sulphur dioxide in the air and are now providing information on the range and intensity of acid rain. They may also in the future be used to determine the extent of agricultural spray drift. In fact, the lichen flora of churchyards provides a uniquely stable and comparable measure of the state of the atmosphere.

Nineteenth-century literature contains many appreciative references to churchyards. It seems to have been widely accepted that the presence of plants and animals contributed greatly to their attractiveness. When the vicar in Wordsworth's 'The Excursion' tells the sad story of Ellen, he and the poet sit in a pleasant spot in the churchyard:

A long stone-seat, fixed in the Churchyard wall;
Part shaded by cool sycamore and part
Offering a sunny resting-place.

Francis Kilvert made many observations later in the century about the people and animals frequenting churchyards and took evident pleasure in their flora. At Langley Burrell in Wiltshire early on the first Sunday in May 1871, he wrote in his diary:

A hot air balloon, seen drifting over the churchyard of St Mary, Braemore, in Hampshire, in mid-June. The air was full of swifts, which were feeding their young in nests under the eaves of this ancient Saxon church, where the horseshoe bat has also been seen.

Dandelions, ribwort plantain and dog rose growing at the base of the church wall, St Margaret's, Cley next the Sea, Norfolk, in late August. Roses both wild and cultivated grow plentifully in churchyards, providing beauty and scent in summer and haws for the birds in winter. In Cheshire, the dog rose is known as brid briar (bird-briar).

I went into the churchyard under the feathering larch which sweeps over the gate. The ivy-grown old church with its noble tower stood beautiful and silent among the elms with its graves at its feet. Everything was still. No one was about or moving and the only sound was the singing of birds. The place was all in a charm of singing, full of peace and quiet sunshine. It seemed to be given up to the birds and their morning hymns. It was the bird church, the church among the birds. I wandered round the church amongst the dewy grass-grown graves and picturesque ivy and moss hung tombstones. Round one grave grew a bed of primroses. Upon another tall cowslips hung their heads.

In Bredwardine churchyard, a few years later, Kilvert wrote: 'some of the graves were white as snow with snowdrops', taking especial pleasure in these first flowers of spring, which now as then are arguably at their finest in churchyards.

Kilvert admired and appreciated nature and loved the familiar plants. Not for him the preoccupation of a modern botanist identifying, say, one of the many tricky species of *Hieracium* (hawkweed) nor was he, as Wordsworth put it, 'One that would peep and botanize / Upon his mother's grave.' (Though Wordsworth could have done with a botanist at his own graveside, for it was planned, so the story goes, that the lesser celandine, his favourite plant, should be carved on his tomb; but the plant which appears on his gravestone is not the lesser but the greater celandine, a plant quite different in appearance).

We have reason to be grateful to those erudite clergymen who extended the boundaries of our knowledge in every branch of natural history from the sixteenth century onwards. Almost any page of any county flora contains an example of the contribution made by such clergymen of international fame or of minor local repute. Even those who, like John Ray, worked on a large conceptual scale and who travelled widely not only in Britain but in the rest of Europe, kept an eye on the natural history of the churchyard. In *The Flora of Suffolk* we find small scabious (now rather rare but still found in churchyards) first recorded in Suffolk by the Revd Sir John Cullum in 1773, and a scarce introduced plant, birthwort, observed in the grounds of the abbey at Bury St Edmunds in the late nineteenth century by the Revd William Hind. One of the most interesting of the botanist-clergy

*The closed buds are
yellow-green, shaded
pink-lilac.*

*Small black beetles
crawling over the
flowers.*

*Field scabious, flourishing in the
churchyard of St Michael's in Idbury,
Oxfordshire, where the grass is cut
only three times a year. These flowers
were painted in late July. (Life size).*

was the Revd Professor John Henslow, who in 1837 stepped aside from a
brilliant academic career as Professor of Botany at Cambridge to become
rector of one of the most backward parishes in Suffolk. In the course of
numerous reforms undertaken at Hitcham, he began to teach botany to the
village children. Doubtless he took the children into the churchyard to
show them the plants. Hitcham churchyard today is well-mown and
contains many lawn plants such as daisy and slender speedwell, but some
attractive meadow species still manage to survive – scabious, dog daisy and
lesser burnet saxifrage, and the yellow flower spikes of common agrimony,
which is also known as church-steeple. If you are lucky, I was told, you may
see a common lizard sunning itself on a gravestone.

Henslow would have known about the difficulties of keeping a
large churchyard in an orderly condition and been interested too in
conserving its flora. It is clear that some difficulties encountered by present-
day incumbents are not new. An ancient legend describes St Patrick
watching a woman pulling nettles in the churchyard to make broth, and in

churchwardens' accounts from the fifteenth century there are payments for 'weding within the Churche yerde' and 'cuttyng downe of the Netylles and Wedes'. Similarly the nineteenth-century accounts of the parish of Hook (now in Humberside) show a fairly considerable outlay on nettle pulling and, towards the end of the century, for mowing the churchyard.

   The problems of reaching an acceptable standard of orderliness remain much the same today, but there is now a wider choice of ways to deal with them. In some churchyards people continue with the old methods. Hay is still made and, occasionally, sold in a few churchyards, and grazing is coming back into fashion. I was told of a churchyard where the vegetation is clipped from the awkward spots close to headstones and between graves by hand, using a pair of sheep-shears. There are a surprising number of churchyards in which an area of ground is deliberately kept as a small nature reserve. At the other extreme, I have seen churchyards covered by the barest fuzz of grass, mown every week, even during drought conditions. Weed-killers, rotary mowers and grass strimmers should be considered only with extreme caution, for they all too easily become the dominating factor in churchyard maintenance. On their account, graves are flattened, gravestones removed and, in their wake, little natural life remains. The celebrated horticulturist J.C. Loudon wrote early in the nineteenth century: 'Churchyards and cemeteries are scenes not only calculated to improve the morals and the taste, and by their botanical riches to cultivate the intellect, but they serve as historical records.' It would be a tragedy if the practices of the late twentieth century were to destroy the rich nature of 'God's Acre'.

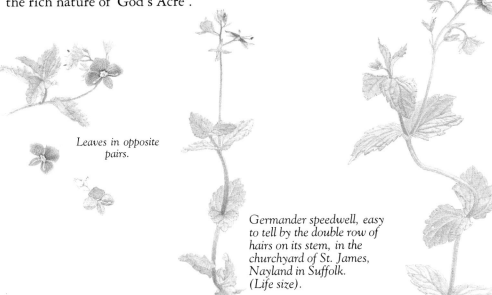

Leaves in opposite pairs.

Germander speedwell, easy to tell by the double row of hairs on its stem, in the churchyard of St. James, Nayland in Suffolk. (Life size).

43

CHURCHYARD FAMILIARS

Wall flowers are bright in their beds
*   And their scent all pervading,*
Withered are primroses heads
*   And the hyacinth fading*
*   But flowers by the score*
*   Multitudes more*
Weed flowers and seed flowers and mead flowers our
*   paths are invading.*

John Betjeman: *Wantage Bells*

THERE ARE CHURCHYARDS AND CHAPELYARDS the length and breadth of England and Wales, in every imaginable setting: high on hills and isolated tors, on moors, in woods, farmland and river valleys, and on all kinds of soil from chalk or limestone to heavily acid conditions and even on solid rock — there is one churchyard in Wales where graves are not dug but blasted with dynamite. Each of these different environments has its own recognizably different flora and fauna. Is it feasible therefore, to think in terms of the plants and animals typical of churchyards? I believe that it is: in a sense churchyards can be regarded as special environments in themselves. Because they have developed a distinctive identity built around certain predictable elements they tend to have more in common with each other than with the land surrounding them. There are certain regional differences, but the overall picture is remarkably consistent.

The churchyards of England and Wales are predominantly grassy even in towns (unlike those on the continent, which are often paved, concreted over or gravelled) and those churchyards which have not been over-mown, or treated with weed-killer or fertilizer, exhibit the rich flora and fauna of unimproved grassland. Within a comparatively small area churchyards may contain an unusually large number of different habitats. The grass in less frequented spots may be cut or grazed only rarely during the year, giving a meadow-like habitat; verges and sometimes wide expanses of grass are often mown hard and frequently, like a garden lawn. Other places may be more or less left to themselves, forming patches of scrub. Paths, walls and boundaries support the flora of wayside and hedgerow. The walls of the church, and memorial stones of various kinds of elaboration harbour plants, insects, small mammals and birds. In or near many churchyards there is water providing an additional marshy or riverside habitat. There may be the typical flora of the woodland from which a churchyard was originally claimed and finally, there is a rich introduced flora ranging from tiny grave plants to large specimens of indigenous and exotic trees.

The variety and number of animals are determined by the size and nature of territory each requires. A churchyard which has an above-average diversity of habitats contains a quite remarkable amount of animal life. Even in an ordinary parish churchyard there is a surprising number of birds and mammals, both resident and visiting, a wide range of insects, and a higher-than-average representation of reptile and invertebrate life.

*Two-spot ladybird on forget-
me-not (life size).*

Ancient meadowland which supports a richly diverse flora is a habitat which is fast disappearing. A few sites have been designated national or local Conservation Trust nature reserves, but most have already been turned into 'improved pasture', which instead of being left to renew itself is ploughed, fertilized and sown with a restricted range of grasses. Nowhere was the difference between the old and the new style of managing grassland more striking than at Morwenstow in Cornwall, where St Morwenna's churchyard stands adjacent to 'improved pasture'. The churchyard, while extremely pretty, is no richer in species than many another in Cornwall. In May, when I made my visit, it was colourful with the last of the daffodils, lesser celandine, primroses, pignut, yarrow, forget-me-not, lesser dog violet, red campion and many other flowers in bloom, while over the wall there was none of these, not a violet, not even a daisy in sight.

All over England and Wales the sites which meadow wild flowers colonize today are hedgebanks, strips of land by rivers and the few remaining 'meadows of delight'.

Forget-me-nots of many kinds are to be found in churchyards. This one (life size), growing on a grave in early May at St Mary the Virgin in Martlesham, Suffolk, seems to be a garden variety of the wood forget-me-not.

Meadow flowers and grasses in Stoke-by-Nayland churchyard, Suffolk. In mid-June, the ox-eye or dog daisies are a dazzling white against the green grass and grey tombs. Common sorrel, ribwort plantain and hawkweed are also to be seen here among crested dog's tail grass, and meadow grass, foxtail and Holcus species.

48

There are now very few meadows which we can enjoy as Shakespeare did,
but there are countless churchyards which contain a wide range
of meadow flowers:

When daisies pied and violets blue
And lady-smocks all silver white
And cuckoo-buds of yellow hue
Do paint the meadows with delight
The cuckoo then, on every tree,
Mocks married men; for thus sings he
  Cuckoo,

[*Love's Labour's Lost*]

May-time daisies,
St Mary,
Wareham, Dorset.

49

Shakespeare's 'daisies pied' were not a special variety: in the seventeenth century 'pied' simply denoted contrast. Shakespeare appreciated the beauty in everyday things, especially the daisy with its delicate drama of colours— the white, crimson-tipped outer florets set around the golden centre. When a survey of churchyards carried out in the county of Suffolk was put on computer, there was only one plant common to them all. One might have expected this to be the daisy, but it seems that this species, which is essentially a plant of grazed grassland and latterly of lawns, has not found a place in the very overgrown churchyards. In fact, the ribwort plantain was the only plant which was found everywhere.

The 'violets blue' of Shakespeare's song are the deliciously scented sweet violets which abound in churchyards (though less in the north and far south-west and not at all in central Wales). Some of the sweet violets in churchyards have larger flowers than usual, which may indicate that they are a garden sort which has become naturalized or cross-bred with the wild species. There is also a recognized hybrid which is altogether a more vigorous plant, with larger leaves as well as flowers. The colour of the flowers is generally in the blue-lilac-purple spectrum, but a common variant is white with a purplish spur. The most widespread and common violet of England and Wales is the common dog violet, though it is not so prevalent in churchyards as outside them, possibly because it seems to favour woodland sites. It was no surprise to find the biggest patches in partly-wooded churchyards or under large boundary trees. The effect of a purple pool of colour is quite arresting, as the flowers present themselves more openly than the sweet violet (the traditional 'shy violet').

The petals of the 'lady-smock' or cuckoo flower shade from a deep pink to Shakespeare's silver white. I was impressed by both their prevalence and persistence. Almost all the churchyards I visited in the spring had a few of these delicate and attractive plants. Some colonies were surviving frequent and regular mowing, but the plants were smaller and less numerous and evidently suffering under this treatment. I know of one instance of complete extinction where a group of about a dozen

Sweet violets growing at the base of the church wall, Holy Trinity, Boxted, Suffolk, in late April. (Life size).

50

'Cuckoo-spit' – foam produced by leafhopper larvae (right).

Sepals turn from yellow-green to ochre with pink-brown tips.

Flowers are palest when first open, becoming deeper lilac, and with veining more pronounced.

Lady's smock (cuckoo flower), one of the prettiest and most characteristic churchyard plants, at Holy Trinity, Boxted, Suffolk, in April. (Life size).

plants was mowed every week from February to late autumn for three years. During the dry weather of the spring of 1984 even the grass succumbed. The only plant that remained green was the diminutive mouse-ear hawkweed, its silvery-haired rosettes of leaves pressed close to the ground lower even than the low set of the mower.

Dialect dictionaries and country glossaries agree that Shakespeare's 'cuckoo-bud' is the bulbous buttercup. It is early-flowering and comes into bloom along with the lady's smock. It too is found in almost every churchyard. Even in Devon and Cornwall and in Wales where this species is less common, it occurs in well over half the churchyards and chapelyards surveyed. In Suffolk, the County Recorder for botany has gone so

51

A species-rich piece of turf: snowdrops with primrose, barren strawberry, celandine and dandelion leaves at All Saints churchyard, Over Worton, Oxfordshire, in late February. (Life size).

far as to make a special mention of churchyards as a particular habitat for this buttercup, as he does also for another spring-flowering kind, the goldilocks, which blooms soon after the bulbous buttercup. In churchyards as elsewhere, the goldilocks buttercup is generally the less common of the two though it is possibly under-recorded. This wiry plant with its inconspicuous, rather short-lived flowers (often missing several petals) is certainly worth looking for in churchyards, especially in slightly shaded areas under trees where it seems to grow especially well. In Cambridgeshire churchyards I saw the best examples of this species that I have ever come across and have since learned that distinct local forms occur in certain churchyards (though banished from the country around them).

Many of the characteristic plants of meadows, including some of the rarer species, can be found in church and chapel yards. One of the prettiest, and one which I had not expected to see so often, is meadow saxifrage. It seems to be able to cope with a variety of churchyard conditions. I have seen tall plants growing up among high grasses and dog daisies in Oxfordshire, and surviving several years of close mowing at Kedington in Suffolk where, though it does not flower, the leaves appear every year by the side of the main path to the church. Though it looks so delicate with its flat rosette of leaves and its soft greeny-white flowers, meadow saxifrage seems to be able to survive an occasional dose of herbicide. The stronghold of meadow saxifrage is East Anglia, but there are churchyard records of it from many counties from as far north as Yorkshire, to the far south-west, where it is believed to be introduced. In Wales it is found only inland, in the mid-south and in a few places in north Wales and Anglesey. It would be interesting to know how many of the sites on record for this plant are churchyards.

The cowslip is perhaps the best known meadow flower and its religious associations have earned it the country name, St Peter's keys. The legend is that St Peter once dropped the keys of heaven and the first cowslips grew up where they fell. (Old-fashioned keys, St Peter's emblem, resemble cowslips rather more than modern ones.) These flowers have a very wide distribution in churchyards, (though they do not occur in those which are very overgrown) and they are subject to many interesting colour variations. I have twice seen in churchyards the rare deep crimson cowslip with a golden throat which cottage gardeners call Devon Red, but there is a range of colour from the golden yellow of the typical plant to a deep apricot with various throat markings. The churchyard of St John the Baptist in the centre of the village of Hartwell in Northamptonshire, keeps its grass well-groomed, but the gardener obviously takes care to avoid mowing groups of wild flowers such as lady's smocks and primroses and most conspicuously, a group of delightful cowslips which were red, pale pink, rich orange and buttery yellow. Such colour variations are thought to be the result of a cross-breeding between the cowslip and the garden polyanthus.

One of the best meadow habitats I have ever seen is at the church of Little Tew, Oxfordshire. At midsummer, the front and one side of the churchyard are tidily mown, though still fairly rich in plants. A corn dolly, symbol of the earth's fertility, hanging on the west wall in the church, clearly presides over the remainder of the churchyard. There I found a flowery paradise, dominated by waist-high dog daisies with meadow saxifrage, red clover, lesser trefoil, and meadow vetchling flourishing in

Startled blackbird in the ivy, at St John the Evangelist, Little Tew, Oxfordshire, in February.

53

Celandines growing in the grass
between gravestones at Cilgwyn,
Dyfed. (Life size).

Weevil
(life size).

The flowers open in the
sunlight, and close in the shade
or at night. The lower side of the
petals is green-tinged.

The glossy yellow
pales almost to silver
as the flowers age.

Millipede
(life size).

among them. Above their level, plants such as horehound and foxglove, naturalized lilies, great willowherb and purple-black columbines made taller contours. Two spicily scented sweetbriars arched gracefully over the high chest tombs, and the boundary hedge and the trees just beyond were full of birds – chaffinches, a blackbird and a song thrush singing to the background murmur of a woodpigeon.

The plant diversity in meadow churchyards in its turn supports a variety of other creatures. My explorations have often disturbed mallards grazing and searching out insects and other invertebrates in the grass. Where churches were originally manorial foundations, the nearby manor house has often become a farm, and ducks and geese enter the churchyard from that or a neighbouring farmyard. At Chesham in Buckinghamshire, ducks fly to the church from ornamental water gardens about a quarter of a mile away, but in some cases, such as at Kedington, it is not at all clear where they come from. Like the wild ducks who also visit churchyards they recognize a good feeding ground.

Ducks purposefully crossing the High Street in Bishop's Castle in Shropshire to graze in the churchyard of St John the Baptist.

I was pleased to find that churchyards also provide both food and occasional nesting places for the grey partridge; at Berrington in Shropshire, a pair made their nest on a game-keeper's grave. The grey partridge is a native bird that has been declining in numbers for several years. Current agricultural practices, such as stubble-burning and autumn ploughing, are a threat to this species, but the application of herbicides and pesticides which kill or poison its food has been particularly destructive. Churchyard surveys record partridges nesting in various parts of England (for their distribution is widespread, if in places very thin), but it was not until July, late in the season, that I came across a whole family of partridges feeding in a churchyard. They were at Westfield in Norfolk, where turtle doves crooned in the trees, and another frequenter of rural churchyards, the yellowhammer, was in full song.

Sometimes, while I sat on a gravestone making notes, I could hear the high notes of a shrew, and a rabbit once came out to feed about three feet away from where I sat. During my explorations, I was continually surprising wild rabbits, which would bound off into the undergrowth or out of the churchyard. At Hauxton, south of Cambridge, where the River Cam winds through pollarded willows just below the lovely, tile-roofed church, a brown and white domestic rabbit, which was clearly in the habit of visiting from a nearby garden, noted my arrival in the churchyard without much concern. Some people become extremely agitated about rabbits in tidy churchyards, largely in vain, because it is virtually impossible to keep rabbits out. I was told of a churchwarden in Shropshire who waged constant war on the rabbit population to the end of his life. Nevertheless, the rabbits outlasted him and have even been seen hopping about over his grave. He might perhaps have welcomed some assistance from some of the rabbits' natural predators, weasels, a whole family of whom were discovered living in a churchyard shed at Silecroft in Cumbria.

These rabbits were sitting among the graves at St Margaret's, Binsey, Oxfordshire.

I only once saw a hare in a churchyard, and that scudded off out of sight in an instant. However, surveys show that hares regularly visit churchyards throughout rural England and Wales. Hedgehogs are frequently observed visiting or living in churchyards, where they find a plentiful supply of slugs, beetles, caterpillars, and other creatures. Moles, which thrive best in permanent pasture, find an almost ideal habitat in churchyards.

There are a few reports of foxes having made their earths inside churchyards, (cemeteries, which are usually larger, appear to be preferred). However, churchyards, both urban and rural, are patronized by foxes as feeding grounds. In tall grass, they find their favourite prey, the field vole, distinguished by its chestnut back, from the greyish bank vole – more an animal of scrub and hedges, and also very acceptable food for a fox. Churchyards also provide foxes with rabbits, wood mice and worms and, in hard times, moles and shrews.

Bank vole, found dead in a churchyard ditch, Suffolk.

Badgers, like rural foxes, are susceptible to disturbance by human beings and will move their set if bothered, but there are several records of badgers inhabiting country churchyards which have plenty of cover and where there is little human activity. They are omnivorous and eat a wider diversity of foods than a fox, but the single most important item of diet is the earthworm, though small mammals, frogs, grubs, beetles, nuts, clovers and grasses all form part of their fare. It is not unusual for churchyards to contain all these and so they are often regular foraging places for badgers. Well-worn paths may be seen criss-crossing the churchyards that they frequent.

Many species of butterfly are to be found in good numbers, especially where there are flowering shrubs and meadow flowers, and where the grass is not cut too short by rotary mowing machines which destroy the eggs and caterpillars. I was visiting churchyards when I saw my first brimstone of the year (the earliest butterfly) and I was pleased to find at my local church (where there are abundant flowering shrubs, wild flowers, and tall grasses) many other species, some of which I would normally travel some distance to see. As well as harbouring burnet moths in late summer, the knapweed is a favourite with marbled white butterflies. Once, I found a perfect chestnut-brown small skipper sunning itself on a bramble, its wings tipped up in the typical pose of that species. The hedge brown (or gatekeeper), wall brown, meadow brown and speckled wood were all nearby. Most of the blues frequent churchyards, though they are less common than the gaily-coloured small tortoiseshell and peacock, which often hibernate in churches and memorials, or in the churchyard trees.

In a typical meadow community, there is a balance of wild flowers and grasses. If a meadow remains ungrazed or unmown, its character changes, and larger plants, such as cow parsley, hogweed, shrubs and young

trees take over. When cow parsley comes into flower all around a church, it makes a breathtaking sea of lacy white. Two cow parsley churchyards stand out in my mind, one surrounding the pretty flint and tile church at Great Waldringfield in Suffolk, wonderfully unruly, and the other at Church Enstone in Oxfordshire.

In searching for a way to describe such luxuriantly overgrown churchyards, I recalled that vernacular names for wild plants include many with the prefix 'dog'—as in dog daisy, the wild ox-eye—simply indicating a larger version of the normative type. In this sense, Great Waldringfield might be termed a 'dog churchyard'. It is surrounded by large trees, well-grown common limes and horse chestnuts, which hold a thriving rookery of fifty nests or more, and the April air is full of cawing. There are sycamores with flaking bark and large shining, blush-pink buds, and tangles of overgrown forsythia. In and around the mists of tall cow parsley I found nettles, rough grasses, foxgloves, red dead-nettle, and bright naturalized double daffodils with thick, sturdy stems.

At Church Enstone, a path runs the whole length of the churchyard from a far gate. On the right, a jungle of cow parsley grows very high under the yew, ash and lime trees. Here and there a headstone is visible, but it is impossible to make a way through the undergrowth without falling over concealed kerbstones or into a ditch. Most of the smaller meadow species have disappeared but more robust plants, such as a great purple patch of dame's violet and some yellow foxglove (presumably spread from a grave-planting), were blooming healthily when I visited the churchyard. I should add, perhaps, that the parishioners may enter the churchyard by an altogether more decorous approach, where two brilliant laburnums frame the lych-gate and a rose twines up from a mat of garden *Helxine* (baby's tears) by the church porch.

As summer comes, cow parsley gives way to hogweed as the dominant plant, and there are tall patches of columbine and hemp agrimony. It is easy to see why botanists rather disapprove of churchyards such as these, in which the interesting small plants representative of the flora of ancient grassland will have been lost. Overgrown churchyards correspond more to a scrub habitat, which has its own benefits for wildlife and is usually well-populated by birds and mammals.

Six-spot burnet moth, sketched at St Andrews, Rufus Castle, Portland, Dorset. (Life size).

58

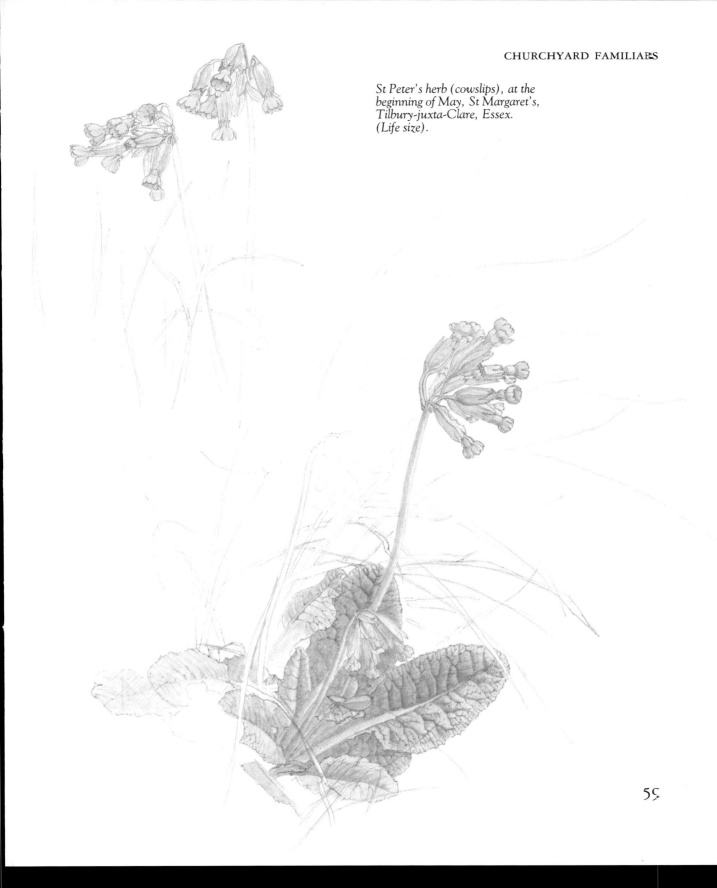

*St Peter's herb (cowslips), at the
beginning of May, St Margaret's,
Tilbury-juxta-Clare, Essex.
(Life size).*

Hedges, shrubs and self-seeded trees are usually luxuriant in overgrown churchyards, and provide shelter and food for birds. The robin and the wren, 'God's cock and hen' in the old rhyme, are two of the most familiar of the churchyard birds. It is unusual to enter a churchyard without disturbing at least one wren. Reclusive by nature, wrens will rocket out of view immediately into whatever cover is handy, while robins, bolder in their behaviour, will flutter in full view from one perch to another,

Robins at St Giles,
Hampton Gay,
Oxfordshire, in January.

adopting that characteristic, quizzical attitude quite as readily on top of a headstone as on the traditional garden spade. They will also make their nests more publicly than other birds. I was told of one that continually nested (unsuccessfully) beneath a leaning gravestone, while a pair at Ashill in Norfolk made their nest in a flower arrangement in the church porch.

A tree frequently planted in churchyards, the common lime, is well known for the wealth of suckers that grow around the lower trunk. If they are not clipped, the trees produce a lush screen of foliage over a dense, tangled frame of twigs, the ideal home for wrens. There was a splendidly unclipped lime beside the impressive parish church of St John the Baptist at Cirencester. Like most town churchyards, this one was municipally maintained, but it was very far from that point of shorn monotony reached by the tidiest parks and churchyards. Several other large trees apart from the great lime were leafy from top to base, and although the mowing was evidently regular and frequent, there were patches which had not been over-tended. Despite ugly signs of weed-killer here and there, an imaginative mix of *laissez-faire* and planting made this a most agreeable green place in the middle of the town.

Wrens also use thick ivy as cover for their nests, principally on boundary walls, since increasingly those responsible for the maintenance and insurance of parish churches refuse to countenance ivy on towers or church walls and insist on its being torn down. Whether opposition to ivy on buildings proceeds from superstition or reason is a matter of debate in many a parish. Blackbirds, song thrushes and finches are attracted to dense ivy as a nesting place, a fact that is also appreciated by many a churchyard cat. Blackbirds are so open in their behaviour, it would be a dull place where you failed to see one, dipping a crocus-coloured beak into the church compost heap, searching for insects in the grass, scuffling in the dark recesses of low trees and shrubs, or singing lustily from a tree.

The churchyard song thrush usually chooses the tallest trees from which to deliver the loud, sweet repetitions of its song. Our local church celebrated Ascension Day in 1984 with a John Dunstable sung mass. It was a blissfully warm, still May evening, and the west door was thrown open, letting in the sunset and allowing the notes of a song thrush to mingle with the plainsong.

A common sight in almost any churchyard, a song thrush using the kerbstone of a grave as its 'anvil' for breaking snails.

Pied wagtails skipping across mown lawns and enjoying puddles on the paths are among those species I encountered over and again in churchyards. Spotted flycatchers use the headstones of graves as places from which to dart after insects. They seem to be birds for which people form a special affection—many churchyard observers mentioned them. Starlings are nearly always to be found nesting in niches in church masonry, often in the towers. They will also try to nest inside the church if they can.

Jackdaws often nest in churches and appear to be particularly attracted to square towers. They also use the high features of church architecture from which to spy out the land for food. There is a Norwich weather adage: 'When three daws are seen on St Peter's/Then we're sure to have bad weather'. The crow family figures in folklore mainly as a symbol of doom, but I know of only one saying of this kind attached to the jackdaw and since it is a sociable creature, it is unlikely that many fatalities follow the sighting of a solitary jackdaw, said to presage death.

The homely sparrow is the inspiration for Bede's haunting image of the transience of human life — as it flies from whence who knows into the great hall, and departs again who knows where. This chirpy associate of humankind is to be found only in well frequented places. As one would expect, sparrows are readily to be found in town centres or in the bustle of a village, but where churches are remote or rarely used they have left or failed to arrive. Perhaps the presence or absence of these little birds, which followed Montgomery and the Eighth Army into the desert on campaign, but which soon abandon a farmhouse left empty, ought to form part of the calculation as to whether or not a church should be made redundant!

Ivy is a good plant for wildlife all the year round, particularly for birds. The importance of dense ivy as a safe wind-proof roost for thrushes and finches is often overlooked, and its abundant winter berries provide fare that is appreciated by the occasional overwintering blackcaps and, more commonly, by finches and thrushes (including winter migrants such as bramblings, redwings, and fieldfares).

Snowdrops and aconites under the giant sycamore at St Peter's, Steeple Aston, Oxfordshire, in February. This churchyard, with its wooded surroundings, is a good place to see birds such as jays. The sycamore itself, more than sixty-six feet high, is taller than the church tower, and its girth is about twenty-three feet.

Churchyards with abundant shrubs, wild flowers and grasses are full of seeds and berries in late autumn and winter and a boon to birds. Summer migrants frequent churchyards along with the resident population. The warbler I came across most frequently was the willow warbler and often heard the silvery falling cadences of this species among the foliage of some tree or high hawthorn hedge. Rambling hedges or large wildernesses of bramble, hawthorn and elder provide good nesting places for whitethroats and other warblers. Dunnocks sing from hedges both high and low, and in spring it seems that there is a cuckoo within earshot of almost every country churchyard.

Dunnock (hedge sparrow) searching for food on a gravel path at St Andrew's in Sherborne St John, Hampshire, in February.

Stout boundary hedges attract finches. It is not unusual to hear the half-lazy, half-urgent call of the greenfinch (a great colonizer of churchyards) or the breezy down-scale song of the chaffinch. If they are bounded by hedges, even the sprucest churchyards have their birds. At Cardinham in Cornwall, the neat grounds of the Methodist Church rise to a closely mown grass bank with a hedge, where I watched nesting chaffinches feeding on some dandelion heads that had managed to bolt up and seed between mowings.

Several species of trees seed themselves—principally ash, sycamore, elder and holly, although I have also seen plenty of rowan, oak and yew, but the seedlings rarely make full growth. Rowan and yew seem to fail of their own accord after about a year's growth. Ash and sycamore are often cut to ground level as saplings. They subsequently form several trunks and emerge as a dense coppice tree. Ash specimens of this kind form a very shapely and attractive ornament to the churchyard. They are often left to grow for several years before being cut again and where there is room, they are sometimes allowed to attain considerable size. These coppice trees make good cover for finches and wrens.

Where a mower is steered around a tree or sapling, other plants take advantage of the respite and form a thick island of vegetation. Woody nightshade, a low grower when left to itself in the shade of churchyard trees and not very significant in hedges, seems to come into its own when scrambling eight or nine feet up hollies—often in association with brambles, which it leaves behind in its climb. Red campion, white bryony and stitchwort will grow round the edge of the island, often out of a huge cushion of flowering bramble, and yarrow will reach its full flowering height. Similar vegetation occurs where mowing ends on the margin of some churchyards, and here in the rough turf you quite commonly come across white comfrey. Common and Russian comfrey are also recorded from churchyards, but it is the white which is the characteristic species, perhaps because it prefers slightly drier conditions.

Two or three tree species will sometimes entwine with each other. At Tring Baptist Church in Hertfordshire, elder, ash, sycamore, yew and ivy grow together in an extraordinary patchwork of foliage. Only two miles away on a summer day, at St Bartholomew's, Wigginton, I picked a very sweet red gooseberry from a bush growing inside a holly which was itself closely intertwined with an ash. Elder and gooseberry are both adept at making use of any suitable habitat: I have seen elders growing out of a fork in a churchyard sycamore and a gooseberry out of a poplar. There were far more members of the currant family than I had expected to find, but while one frequently encounters small gooseberry bushes flowering and fruiting on graves, blackcurrants are a little less common. I have even come upon a few feral red currants. Currant plants in churchyards are undoubtedly sown by birds. The seeds germinate in crevices where they have either been left when birds have wiped their beaks after feasting in nearby farms or gardens, or where they have been deposited in birds' droppings.

At the other end of the scale from the scrubby wilderness is the 'lawn' or, in extreme cases, 'bowling-green' churchyard. In general, there is at least a small area, usually on either side of the path from the lych-gate to the porch, which is kept well shorn. Some entire churchyards are like this, but they are so far in the minority. Not surprisingly, lawn-like conditions give rise to the flora associated with garden lawns, but in some cases the incidence of certain species is remarkable. The pretty little slender speedwell which forms mats of delicate blue, is known to have been increasing in lawn habitats, but nowhere more so, it seems, than in churchyards. I saw it almost everywhere and received letters from botanists throughout England and Wales remarking on its colonizing vigour. Another plant which is really rather rare, but seems to occur fairly often in churchyards is

Turf with moss and willowherb seedlings all bound up together at All Saints, Fulham, London, in February. (Life size).

keeled cornsalad, an inconspicuous annual with forked branches, rather narrow leaves arranged in pairs on opposite sides of the stem, and a head of tiny mauve flowers. It tends to grow in the lee of headstones or by walls, just out of reach of the mower.

Most lawn plants are perennials and hug the ground in a rosette of leaves, like the daisy, which thrives in grass that is closely mown. Yarrow manages to survive, flowering as and when it can—its dark, feathery leaves are usually to be found even in a close-cut sward. Mouse-ear hawkweed is familiar not only on closely mown lawns and banks but also on the raised mounds of graves, a micro-habitat in themselves. Field wood-rush is also common here. A small plant with narrow leaves lightly fringed with long hairs, it brings forth its tiny clusters of nut-brown flowers as early as March. The handsome downy, greyish-green rosette of wide leaves belonging to the hoary plantain is easy to spot in short grass from the earliest months of the year. If it has a rest from mowing, it comes into flower from May to August with the palest of pink blooms, very showy for a plantain; in fact, in St Andrew's churchyard at Great Rollright, Oxfordshire the brush-like flower was so dense that I mistook it from a distance for a small, pale orchid.

Burnet saxifrage can sometimes be discerned among the grasses, looking like a rather darker, coarser version of the salad burnet. This plant lies low until late summer, when it puts up its flowering stem with great speed. In meadow conditions, it will grow to a height of over three feet but I have several times found its white umbrella heads of flowers on stems only five or six inches high, dotted all over flat-mown grass.

Some of the most familiar plants of churchyards are those inherited from woodland. Churchyards such as Milland St Luke's in the middle of Woolmer Forest in Hampshire or St Michael, Penkival, on the slope of a gloriously wooded Cornish valley, are relatively few, but many of our churchyards were originally carved out of woods and forests. Now, even in places where the village has become a town and the countryside has receded, the churchyard may retain a relic woodland flora.

One of the most common and evocative woodland plants is the bluebell. Just as in bluebell woods, the flowers can make a glimmering blue mist amongst the green of the grasses and their own leaves. But things are not as simple as they seem. If some plants look different from the others, close inspection may reveal them to be not the native woodland bluebell but

One of the nicest, as well as one of the commonest of churchyard plants: hoary plantain, in June at St Mary's, North Aston, Oxfordshire. (Life size).

Wood sorrel growing in a bank by a chapel at Cilgwyn, Dyfed, in May. (Life size).

Petals are white with delicate pink veining.

Flowers have cream stamens with pinhead anthers.

There is a yellow triangular nectary guide on each petal.

The leaves are hairy.

the so-called Spanish bluebell, a closely related garden species. In the native bluebell the anthers are cream-coloured and the tips of the slender bells arch back. The Spanish bluebell looks more robust, has broader leaves, and the individual flowers have wider bells and blue anthers. Hybrids, which are frequently white or pink, may show almost any combination of these features. They and the Spanish bluebell are very common in churchyards, probably introduced by visitors planting bulbs from a home garden on a grave.

Field wood-rush, at St Meubred, Cardinham, Cornwall, in April. (Life size).

One of the prettiest flowers of ancient woodland, the wood anemone, does not occur as frequently or in such plenty as the invasive bluebell. Wood anemones generally grow in situations which still resemble a woodland habitat, under trees and in association with other woodland plants. There is always a pleasure in finding its starry white flowers with that subliminal flush of pink. The woodland plant most delicate of all in appearance however, is the wood sorrel, which also continues to haunt churchyards. Low-growing, it makes small soft, pale, clover-shaped leaves, from among which rise white flowers exquisitely veined with lilac.

Lesser celandines are a common sight in most churchyards and very welcome in the bleak early months of the year. My records suggest that they tend to come into flower rather earlier than is usual elsewhere, possibly because conditions are often both sheltered and sunny. However, there are also deeply shaded spots, and I have a note for 1984, recording a Hertfordshire celandine in flower in June. The County Recorder for south-east Yorkshire has noted the slightly less common sub-species *bulbifera* (recognizable from the little bulbils at the base of the leaves, and generally narrower petals) growing in several churchyards when it was not found on waysides in the surrounding country. It would be interesting to know if this variant is to be found in churchyards elsewhere.

The grey-green leaves of lady's mantle from a lower part of the stem.

Primroses are plants of both woods and hedgebanks and they thrive in a very large proportion of churchyards in England and Wales. These populations are of mixed descent. Where they grow among a variety of other woodland plants, they are clearly part of the forest origins of the churchyard. However, they are well-loved plants, which have long been planted on graves. The plantings are sometimes of garden provenance, sometimes taken from local wild populations.

The primrose family naturally produces odd forms or 'sports'. I have occasionally found flowers of unusual colours growing far away from gardens and in situations where hybridization with garden primulas seems unlikely. The garden writer and botanist, John Parkinson, writing in 1629, described no less than twenty-one forms of primrose (including cowslips and oxlips), 'all of which kinds' he remarks 'have been found wilde'. New wild forms are still occurring. In 1982, Bressingham Gardens nursery put on the market a delightful, pale pink double primrose which had been discovered in the wild. I have been very struck by the frequent occurrence of a pretty primrose, pinkish in colour, looking as if the palest of plum-coloured washes had been added to its original yellow. In other

Lady's mantle, one of the many species named after the Virgin Mary, flowering at St James, Piccadilly, in London, in July. This is a plant which readily seeds itself.

A single flower (life size).

*The colour is not a true pink,
but a primrose yellow, suffused
with pink.*

*The churchyard 'pink'
primrose, at St Margaret's,
Tilbury-juxta-Clare, Essex,
in April. (Life size).*

respects the plants are the same as the normal form. I found this washed
pink primrose, which I have come to think of as the 'churchyard primrose',
among almost every primrose population of any size, and in many places
where there were no garden polyanthus apparent to create colour hybrids.
Other primrose/polyanthus hybrids occur in a variety of colours, usually
with a slightly less delicate petal texture. Another form of primrose which I
have found several times in churchyards is the rather ungainly form
known as variety *caulescens*, in which the
flowers grow not from single stems rising

from the root but in an umbel of short stems which spring from a single point at the top of a single stout stem. Each sub-stem bears a flower which is just like that of the normal primrose.

There are two rather discreet plants which give a clear indication that the area in which they are growing was originally woodland. The dark green serrated leaves arranged in opposite pairs up the stem of dog's mercury are most easily spotted in February and March, and the plant comes early into spikes of small greenish flowers. Moschatel, or town hall clock, flowers in April and May. Its name comes from the inconspicuous but pretty flower head which presents four almost square 'clock-face' flowers with a fifth flower facing upwards.

Churchyards are the best places to go in the late winter for a glimpse of the first flowers of the year. Only a few weeks after Christmas, the first snowdrops start to appear, closely followed by winter aconites and then lesser celandines and daffodils. The snowdrop, thought to be native in parts of Wales and western England and possibly elsewhere, has been so widely introduced that it would be impossible to identify an aboriginal population without a record of the floral history of a churchyard. It readily becomes naturalized in churchyard conditions and there are many splendid churchyards where both single and double varieties spread over large areas under trees and between the graves. Along with parkland, the churchyard is an important habitat for the winter aconite, which may grow among snowdrops or alone in a brilliant yellow mass. Winter aconites can be difficult to raise, but seem to find churchyard conditions most favourable. I have seen a dozen or so aconites planted on graves double in numbers within only a year or two and spread outside the kerbstones.

Aconites, painted from the large population beneath trees in the church boundary, Drayton Beauchamp, Buckinghamshire, in late February. (Three-quarters life size).

One of the most common naturalized plants is the daffodil, which makes a spectacular spring show in many churchyards. The wild species is smaller and more delicate than any of the garden varieties and, to my mind, much prettier. I have seen and heard of churchyards in several counties where the daffodils seem to be an original wild population, and in Norfolk most of the wild daffodils appear to be found in churchyards. However, daffodils – Lent lilies, as they are still called in some counties – have always been popular flowers, and wild ones were certainly planted on graves in the past. This would account for the cases where daffodils that are to all appearances wild grow in situations in which one would not normally expect to find the wild species. Adding extra diversity, large naturalized populations of garden varieties (some of them interesting old-fashioned kinds) often grow in churchyards. They are fairly robust and persist in less than ideal conditions. A few most exotic garden daffodils, their trumpets a mass of yellow frill, made an odd sight among the wild flowers at Great Waldringfield.

Several of the plant species which are traditionally grown on graves readily become naturalized and spread. Sometimes it takes no more than a bunch of flowers or a wreath laid on a grave to establish a new species in a churchyard. This is the case with flowers like garden lady's mantle and honesty, and may explain the occurrence of some rather rare plants outside their normal habitat or area of distribution. Honesty, which produces the silvery seed pods that find their way into so many church flower arrangements, has become a familiar sight. Occasionally the rare, white honesty, which is fragrant, may have been planted on graves, but the white-flowered kind in churchyards is usually a white form of the common species. At Hawridge churchyard in Buckinghamshire, there is a very odd honesty which has untidy-looking bi-coloured petals (not leaves, as is more usual) splashed with white.

Lungwort is another fairly widespread introduction. This herb may occur in the taller vegetation of churchyard margins, by walls or on graves. The variety most commonly grown has broad leaves with whitish blotches on them, which earned it names such as Virgin Mary's milkdrops and Mary's tears. The way in which the flowers change from pink to blue, both colours (and shades in between) being displayed at the same time, has given rise to a number of biblical composite names such as Josephs and

Lungwort blooms (life size) at St Mary's, Ovington in Essex, in early May. The leaves have light green blotches on a slightly darker green background, and the calyces are covered with dark purple pimples and bristly transparent hairs.

Marys, Children of Israel, Adam and Eve, and Abraham, Isaac and Jacob. Lungwort is also known as Jerusalem cowslip, Bedlam (Bethlehem) cowslip and Good Friday plant (from the time of year it comes into flower). Another member of the borage family which is widely naturalized and more common than lungwort in churchyards is green alkanet, a tall blue-flowered plant with the typical bristly hairs of all borages.

Churchyards reflect the diversity of wild flora which grows in the countryside around them, and this applies to naturalized as well as native species. Winter heliotrope and three-cornered leek are found abundantly in churchyards in Devon and Cornwall, and the drooping star of Bethlehem has even acquired the local name of 'Bodney lily' in the churchyard at Bodney in west Norfolk. In the north of England, the delicately lacy sweet cicely is plentiful around places of human habitation and is believed to be an escape from cultivation. In some churchyards in the Yorkshire Dales it is as abundant as cow parsley in the southern counties.

Cottage garden plants are enjoying renewed interest among gardeners, but they have never been out of fashion in churchyards. Many species planted on graves are brought from local gardens and the introduced plants of the churchyard may be as representative of the domestic flora of the parish as the wild flowers are of the surrounding countryside. Many of them are native wild plants that grow truly wild only in restricted locations or conditions, but have been widely grown in gardens and churchyards. Common Solomon's seal, with its arch of wing-like leaves and creamy flower bells, is a plant of southern woodlands, but it is well established and widespread as an introduction. It shares its churchyard habitat with a hybrid that is the most common garden form. Solomon's seal has had biblical associations since at least the first century AD. Its root is supposed to resemble the seal of Solomon, the magic pentacle which was supposed to point to the five wounds of Christ. It has an alternative English name, 'ladder to heaven' and it is often planted upon graves. In favourable conditions it can spread to form a most attractive small forest of foliage, which arises suddenly as if from nowhere in spring.

Moschatel (or 'town hall clock') is also Good Friday plant, because its greeny blooms appear early in spring about Easter-time.

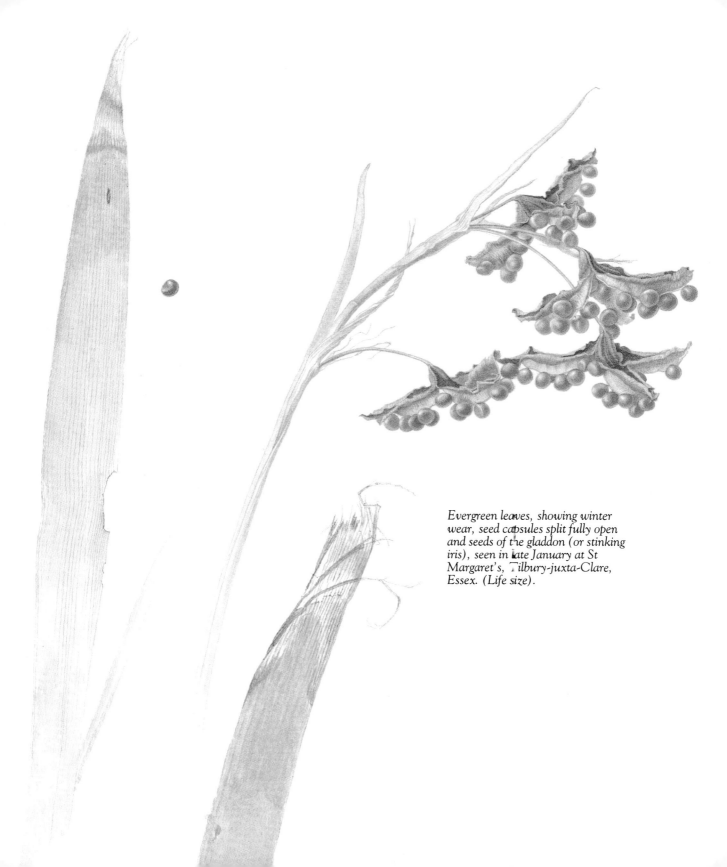

Evergreen leaves, showing winter wear, seed capsules split fully open and seeds of the gladdon (or stinking iris), seen in late January at St Margaret's, Tilbury-juxta-Clare, Essex. (Life size).

During the winter months the bright green spear-shaped leaves and bright orange-red seeds of gladdon, a native iris, are a welcome sight in many churchyards in the south and midland counties. Sometimes the seed-heads are used in flower arrangements for church or graves and the plant's very frequent occurrence must be partly due to this, but I suspect that it is encouraged and perhaps planted in churchyards, as are a number of other evergreen species, their foliage a symbol of life amid death.

Rock may seen an inhospitable habitat, but there are a number of species, both wild and naturalized, which readily colonize the stone habitats that are so plentiful in churchyards if not in the surrounding country. The common houseleek thrives on paved or concreted graves and also on the roofs of porches and lych-gates. It is frequently planted, since it is supposed to bring good luck and give protection against lightning—an important consideration with buildings as high as churches. Another common grave-plant is the large yellow stonecrop whose bright flowerheads make umbrellas above the dense mat of fleshy leaves. A number of the saxifrages, in particular London pride, are also common on graves. Some garden plants such as aubrieta and snapdragons seem to persist on walls long after the original plantings on the ground have been ousted by more strongly growing species. Ivy-leaved toadflax has spread to walls all over Britain since its introduction in the seventeenth century and is now very plentiful.

Several of our familiar native wild flowers are to be found growing on and in the shelter of walls; indeed some of them grow so thickly that the structure beneath can hardly be seen at all. Pellitory-of-the-wall, as its name would suggest, is very common in this situation. George Crabbe makes a mention of it in an early poem:

> Owls and ravens haunt the buildings,
> Sending gloomy dread to all;
> Yellow moss the summit yielding,
> Pellitory decks the wall.

Navelwort, or wall penny-wort, is a typical wall species in the west. Hedgerow plants, such as stitchwort (called Sunday whites in one Devon village) frequently colonize walls, and plantains, sowthistles of all three types and barren strawberry find footholds everywhere.

Ivy-leaved toadflax from the wall of Braemore churchyard, Hampshire. (Life size).

75

Most importantly, churchyard walls are a habitat for ferns, especially in the drier, more easterly counties, where they are generally scarce. The walls of a church, too, are a good habitat, especially near leaking drainpipes and on steps leading down to the crypt or basement, places where there is damp and shade. One of the most familiar and easily recognizable ferns is the common polypody, which also grows on the tiled roofs of churches and lych-gates. Hartstongue fern, with its glossy tongue-like leaves, is another widespread species. The tall neat fronds of male fern grow handsomely at the base of the wall or in damp corners on the north sides of churches. Good specimens will wave triumphantly out of the mower's reach in the narrow gaps between chest tombs. Similar in size, but slightly less common in churchyards is the lady fern, which prefers an acid soil. It has long fronds—with a characteristic droop at the tips—making a large, graceful crown of green.

Three most attractive wall ferns of the genus *Asplenium* make themselves very much at home on church and churchyard walls. Black spleenwort grows in dense, glossy-green tufts. It has about fifteen pairs of leaflets, themselves divided into toothed lobes, descreasing in size towards the tip of each main stem, which is usually curved. The related wall rue grows in more irregular leafy tufts, which look like a scruffier, darker green version of its namesake, rue. Maidenhair spleenwort, like the true maidenhair fern, is altogether more delicate; its forty or so pairs of simple leaflets grow, more or less equal in size, from a thin glossy black stem, and the plant looks like a very large bright green spider. The fronds of the rusty-back fern grow in small, rather stiff clumps, the leaflets slightly cupped and covered with rusty-brown scales on the underside. This plant is mainly associated with the western parts of England and Wales.

Trees possibly do more than any other plants to create the atmosphere of a churchyard. Without them, churchyards are almost invariably bleak and windswept—small plains without any points of reference. Fortunately, only relatively few are like this and many of our churchyards resemble wooded islands set in pasture or arable land, providing shelter and shade.

Yews are the archetypal churchyard tree. They are native in Britain only on well-drained chalk or limestone which indicates that most of the churchyard trees must have been deliberately planted. They are

Male fern, just beginning to unfurl in a chapelyard in Cilgwyn, Dyfed, in spring. (Life size).

SACRED
to the Memory

9 of July 18⁻

ALSO

ANN the daughter died
25 58 years

Herb Robert and hartstongue fern in a grave in St Brynach's churchyard, Nevern, Dyfed. Hartstongue fern quite often colonizes graves in shaded places.

77

present in greater numbers in the west of Britain and also found in Breton churchyards which would suggest a strong Celtic connection. Although it is difficult to age them precisely, some of the churchyard yews are undoubtedly of very great antiquity.

Interestingly the custom of planting yews in holy places is still continued, whatever the reason may have been in the past. The common yew is a protective tree both physically and symbolically: its dense bulk shields the church from wind and weather; in folk belief it gives protection from evil. The yew is also the symbol of immortality and resurrection. There are many medieval references to the decking of churches with yew on Easter Sunday. Even today, it is regarded as a rather special tree. I was quite startled to see in Selborne church during Lent, a very simply fashioned cross of rough-hewn yew branches, placed high before the altar. Outside was the famous ancient churchyard yew, surrounded by a circular bench seat. This tree had the added distinction of supporting two species of lichen—lichens are rather rare on the shiny, flaking bark of yews.

The Windrush Valley from Swinbrook churchyard in late July, with house martins gathering over the churchyard. The pale, dried-up grasses in front of the wall almost hide the gravestones. Pollard willows show the course of the Windrush.

79

Yews were commonly planted by the lych-gate and in some places the priest traditionally met coffins at the yew tree. The records of the parish clerks at Clyst Hydon in Devon contain several references to the planting of yews on graves between 1777 and 1814. At Wateringbury in Kent an epitaph draws attention to a yew tree planted on a grave there in 1597 by a certain Thomas Hood. (This tree measured eleven feet and four inches in girth in 1982).

Most yews planted today are the fastigiate form known as the Irish yew, a natural sport found on the limestone cliffs of County Fermanagh, propagated, and widely distributed. It is a compact tree, used for avenues and small spaces, but continued familiarity with it has not made me like it. I prefer the height, the great tip-tilted branches and the wide skirts of the old yews. The British Trust for Ornithology has records for mistle thrush, greenfinch, chaffinch, linnet, goldcrest and coal tit nesting in yews. They and other observers agree that the fastigiate yew is the more favoured by birds.

Also associated with churchyards are the holly and the rowan. Both are holy trees, with reputed powers of protection against evil; the red berries both trees produce were believed to be particularly effective in this respect. In some places coffins were fashioned out of rowan wood. Like yew, both trees will self-seed and foot-high seedlings of any of these three species are a fairly common sight in churchyards, although holly seedlings seem to be the only ones that are allowed to grow on. I have seen countless small hollies between two and six or seven feet high, but never a rowan or yew at that intermediate stage.

If I had to choose only one plant genus to demonstrate the diversity of churchyard habitats it would be *Geranium*—the cranesbills (not to be confused with the bedding geraniums of gardeners which are classified botanically as *Pelargonium*). There are cranesbills of one kind or another in almost every churchyard habitat. The most widespread is the pink-flowered herb Robert. It can be found beside paths, growing on or at the foot of walls, in banks and shady places and occasionally in the grass sward, and may be in flower from late March right through until October. One of the most cheerful sights of winter is the rosette of filigree leaves, often flame-red at this season, against the dull granite chippings it is now the fashion to spread over graves.

Swifts flying around the church tower, Charlbury, Oxfordshire. They are feeding on the winged insects carried aloft in the updraught.

One of the most attractive species of the churchyard, the meadow cranesbill, grows among the taller grasses in late summer. A typical plant of rough grass verges and field margins (and one which had been adopted into gardens), its wild distribution lies in a wide band down the centre of England, penetrating into the south-east of Wales. It is clearly native in some churchyards, such as St Michael's at Dulas in Herefordshire, and it has been planted in a number of others, in Suffolk, for example. *Gratia Dei* seems to have been a popular name in the sixteenth century, and I can think of no more joyful plant to express thankfulness than this one, with its graceful profusion of sky-blue summer flowers.

Other native *geranium* species to be seen among the churchyard grasses and on overgrown graves include cut-leaved, dove's-foot and small-flowered cranesbills, all with fairly small mid-pink flowers. The handsome purplish-red bloody cranesbill makes shapely hummocks over graves in many West Yorkshire churchyards. As it is native to that region and has been taken into gardens, churchyard plants may be of mixed provenance. At Gayton in Northamptonshire, where bloody cranesbill does not grow in the wild, well-established naturalized plants have long been on record.

A few non-native cranesbills are fairly frequent in churchyards. I saw French cranesbill with its deep pink, veined flowers in a tangle of grasses at Dulas, and it was reported in a number of the churchyard surveys. So, occasionally, was the pencilled cranesbill, an introduced species with pale pink or white flowers lined with dark pink-violet veins. By far the commonest of the introductions, however, is dusky cranesbill with its dramatic, black-purple petals that curve back, away from a contrasting pale centre. The garden name of this plant is 'mourning widow' which might have some connection with its frequency as a grave plant. It grows very handsomely in two London churchyards—St James's, Piccadilly, and St Stephen's in South Kensington. It seems to be most at home in a gardened environment, though there are records of plants that have become naturalized in churchyards in several counties, indicating that it can survive a certain amount of competition from native plants.

One of the prettiest of the cranesbills, and one which illustrates the ambiguous status of some of the churchyard plants, is shining cranesbill.

It has small clear-pink flowers, shining stems, and green
leaves which have a pink tinge to them. Shining cranesbill
is native to many parts of Britain but somewhat patchy in its distribution.
Generally speaking, it is to be found in shady hedgerows among
rocks and on old walls. It also occurs in a number of churchyards. My
records for it include four from churchyards on Exmoor, two from Rutland,
one from Suffolk, one from Lincolnshire and eight from Cardiganshire
(where it was rare fifty years ago), and I have also seen it in North Yorkshire.
However, in the north-west of Yorkshire, where one would expect
it to be wild, the plant I saw was in a stone container by the side of the
porch entrance. I do not know whether it was bird-sown or had been planted
there. In Suffolk, shining cranesbill plants may be native or introduced. It is
not a common flower in that county though it is locally abundant in some
places. At Holton-le-Moor in Lincolnshire, it is known that the
vicar introduced shining cranesbill to the churchyard from Matlock,
Derbyshire, in 1880. Remarkably, the plant still survives there.

*Meadow cranesbill, in early July at
Asthall churchyard, Oxfordshire (life
size), showing buds, flowers and
'crane's-bill' fruits.*

SANCTUARY
and
SURVIVAL

*. . . I stood one evening at the little gate at
Brockenhurst churchyard, and counted between me and
the church twenty gravestones stained with the red alga
{Trentipohlia}, showing a richness and variety of
colouring never seen before, the result of so much wet
weather. For this alga, which plays so important a
part in nature's softening and beautifying effect on
man's work . . . is still in essence a water-plant: the
sun and dry wind burn its life out and darken it to the
colour of ironstone, so that to anyone who may notice the
dark stain it seems a colour of the stone itself; but when
rain falls the colour freshens and brightens as if the old
grey stone has miraculously been made to live.*

W.H. Hudson: *Hampshire Days*

THERE IS A STORY WRITTEN BY the twelfth-century monk, Reginald of Durham, which describes how, on the feast of St Cuthbert, a nobleman was hunting in the border country of Lothian when he chased a fine stag to one of the churches dedicated to St Cuthbert. Crowds of people were celebrating the feast, playing games and dancing in the churchyard. The weary stag had just enough strength to jump the churchyard wall and, as if it knew it was in sanctuary, fled no further, but walked quietly to the church porch and lay down. Neither the hounds nor the huntsmen made any move to enter the churchyard and the people at the festival marvelled, says Reginald, at the way St Cuthbert, who had so loved animals during his life, extended his protection to them after his death. Nobody questioned the right of the stag to sanctuary.

Sadly, the story does not end there. A boy was induced to drive the stag out of sanctuary and, once outside the churchyard, it was set upon and killed. Then, as now, there was a difference between ideals and reality in the protection of wildlife. Five out of the six species of deer that occur in the wild in Britain have been observed in churchyards. In common with a number of other creatures, they find churchyards are welcome but not necessarily vital feeding grounds. However, there are some plants and animals for which the churchyard habitat is of crucial importance and that do in a real sense require sanctuary there.

The importance of churchyards is recognized and well-documented in some counties. The Norfolk Naturalists' Trust's Conservation Scheme has shown that, in Norfolk at least, seven plants (pignut, burnet saxifrage, cowslip, ox-eye daisy, meadow saxifrage, sorrel, and lady's bedstraw) are largely dependent on churchyards. In Ceredigion in Wales, churchyards are the main habitat for hedge bedstraw, yellow oat-grass, quaking grass and green-winged orchid.

Some of the many forms of wildlife under threat in Britain, while not confined to churchyards, can find refuge there. The little fern called adder's tongue, a plant of ancient meadows, is an example to be found in a number of churchyards. Among small mammals, the harvest mouse and the water shrew both find churchyards a useful habitat and the red squirrel, now a rare animal, has been observed feeding in those in remote places. Reptiles and amphibians are everywhere becoming scarcer, but snakes and lizards

Common blue butterflies on the delicate, short-lived flowers of pale flax, at St Andrew's, Rufus Castle, Portland, Dorset. (Life size).

find in churchyards plenty of places in which to live, breed and hibernate. They are occasionally seen basking on the warm stone of graves. Frogs, newts and toads are all to be found, and it is important to preserve their churchyard niche when their other countryside habitats are fast being drained and destroyed. The same applies to butterflies and moths, some of which can find everything needed for the completion of their whole life-cycle in a sensitively managed churchyard. The purple hairstreak butterfly, for instance, can find all it requires in life in and around an oak, even in a small churchyard.

A few national rarities such as yarrow broomrape and tall thrift make exciting additions to the churchyard flora, but equally as interesting are the numerous regional rarities which are to be found in many counties. Churchyards provide habitats that are not otherwise available for a considerable range of plants. The most easterly site for navelwort or wall pennywort is the churchyard wall at Litchborough in Northamptonshire. In Kent, churchyards are almost the only places in which to find the *Asplenium* group of ferns; the same is true in Sussex for rusty-back fern and bladder fern. More than half the British species of lichen grow on stone, but since lowland Britain contains almost no natural outcrops of rock, churchyards provide the only significant areas of old permanent stonework upon which they can grow. This is why churchyards are so important as lichen sanctuaries: essentially because they provide a habitat for those lichens that require a stone base on which to grow. It is not, however, a simple provision; there are infinite subtleties. Church and churchyard walls and memorials are often the most ancient stones in a parish, and the lichens which have colonized them are likewise among the most ancient specimens in the country of these long-lived plants. The church walls themselves have often been modified or cleaned and the lichens disturbed, so church wall lichens are rarely as old as the church itself. Nevertheless they often include species not found on memorials.

Churches are usually built on an east-west axis, and so their walls face more or less due north, south, east and west, and each aspect has its own type of lichen flora. Similarly, the various materials of which churches are built each support a characteristic range of lichens. The lintel and sill stones are often different from the main body of the church, which may be built of stone, flint or bricks. Mortar and concrete, too, provide a site for lichens, as do roofs. Finally, there are memorial stones in a variety of materials—limestone, marble, sandstone, slate and granite—facing in different directions, some in the sun, some shaded. Many types of lichens find homes in the long vertical faces of headstones, the horizontal expanses of chest tombs, and in the crannies of carvings, some of them enriched by the droppings of perching birds.

The lichens which grow on a calcareous substrate such as limestone and marble (when eventually it has weathered) are rather different from those colonizing acid stone. There is generally some variation in the materials used for memorials and headstones, even in parishes where local stone predominates. A lichen survey carried out in the limestone Vale of Glamorgan showed that the fashion for sandstone on graves, which was especially prevalent during the nineteenth century, provided acid-loving lichens with sites that they would not otherwise have found in the area.

Many churchyards are exceptionally rich in lichens. The churchyard at Trotton in West Sussex contains about a hundred species, and forty to fifty are often recorded. The greatest number has been found at Mickleham in Surrey, where no less than one hundred and fifty species were identified on stones and trees in the churchyard.

The fact that there are a number of lichens which are impossibly difficult for the beginner to recognize has kept many people from even attempting to identify members of this interesting and often very beautiful group of plants. Nevertheless many of the species found in churchyards are so distinct in appearance, that with only a little knowledge one can make an informed guess. It is well worth investing in a hand lens (a magnification of ten is adequate) to see the tiny intricacies of these plants more vividly. Sometimes, minute insects can be seen moving, living and feeding on the folds and lobes of the lichens. It is easy to become totally absorbed in the tiny details, as I was one sunny spring morning, when working with a hand lens on a chest-tomb that was particularly rich in lichens, until brought back to the world by the attentions of a churchyard cat which joined me on the tomb, biting and butting for further affection.

Caloplaca flavescens is one of the most eye-catching lichens (which still goes by its old name *C. heppiana* in many field guides). It is a deep, rich orange with the lobes of its margin slightly domed. A near relative *Caloplaca aurantia* is paler and more yellow in colour, with flat, spreading

88

marginal lobes that hug the stone. Both are limestone species, commonly found on the sunny side of headstones. Very old plants may have rosettes several inches across. As the plants age they often die back at the centre, making a circle or semi-circle of orange. In Selborne churchyard, the older gravestones are lit by a mass of such small sunsets. There the colour of the *Caloplaca* is smudged with the cloudy white of the species *Verrucaria hochstetteri*, finely dotted with tiny black fruiting bodies.

On the tops of limestone graves, and sometimes on the older sandstone, where bird droppings have had a nutrifying effect over a long period, grow the nitrogen-hungry lichens. *Physcia caesia* has a very neat bluish-grey rosette and off-white powdery encrustations on the lobes. Very similar, but darker, with a more greenish tinge is *Phaeophyscia orbicularis*, which turns bright green or in some cases, green-brown, when wetted. Another common and distinctive grey species is *Physcia adscendens*, whose marginal lobes are raised and hooded at the tip and bear obvious bristles.

Two species which not only grow on the tops of headstones but also provide bright splashes of orange on stone or brick walls are *Xanthoria parietina* and *X. calcicola* (formerly called *X. aureola*). They are quite alike except that *X. calcicola* has small, crusty, rod-like outgrowths that are absent in *X. parietina*, and fewer of the flat fruiting discs. The lobes of both are more leaf-like than those of the *Caloplaca* species, and there is a simple distinction that removes any doubt: if you can lift the margin of the lichen easily with a finger-nail, it is *Xanthoria*; if the margin is tightly fixed to the stone, it is *Caloplaca*.

This common, greyish-white lichen, Buellia canescens, turns greenish when wet. Painted at West Liss churchyard, Hampshire. (Life size).

Parmelia mougeotii, *a small delicate, yellow-grey lichen, found on sandstone tombs and church walls. (Life size).*

Xanthoria parietina, *a lichen common on gravestones used as bird perches, and quite resistant to air pollution.*

Some lichens may be seen in urban churchyards—certainly those in country towns. In fact in London two-thirds of the lichen flora occurs in old churchyards. But the state of health of lichen flora is related very closely to the quality of the air: the standard test for air pollution is the presence or absence of certain lichens, since different species are quantifiably more or less sensitive to sulphur dioxide. In polluted churchyards where old gravestones once bore a thriving lichen growth, some of the species have managed to survive, though not to expand or form new plants. *Caloplaca flavescens* is still to be found on memorials dating from the eighteenth century in a few London churchyards, though it is absent from most of the big cemeteries established in the nineteenth century. The powdery lichens are commonly found in urban surroundings. *Psilolechia lucidia* coats the damp parts of gravestones and walls with a luminous green sheet, and with its liking for damp, often grows inside the incised lines of a name or epitaph, picking out the words in lichen green. *Lepraria incana*, which grows in a loose soft blue-grey powdery crust, is to be found only on walls and gravestones in dry shady places, as it is unusual in its inability to grow in direct sunlight or rain.

Lecanora conizaeoides is a lichen which positively thrives in polluted conditions. Discovered as late as 1860 and now common all over eastern England, this species is easy to recognize with its grey-green scurfy crust and pale green fruiting bodies with greyish margins. The lichenologist, Francis Rose, describes the fruiting bodies of the *Lecanora* genus and a few other lichens as 'jam tarts' of different kinds, which is of great assistance in distinguishing one species from another. *Lecanora*

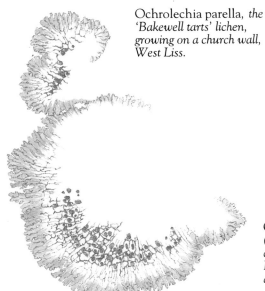

Ochrolechia parella, *the 'Bakewell tarts' lichen, growing on a church wall, West Liss.*

Lecanora atra, *showing the large, distinctive 'blackcurrant jam tarts'.*

Caloplaca flavescens (heppiana) (left), *the orange star lichen. The centre of this one, at West Liss in Hampshire, had disappeared, leaving an arc of orange.*

conizaeoides has 'pale green jam tarts', while those of *L. campestris* are 'milk-chocolate brown tarts'; *L. atra* has large but slightly distorted 'blackcurrant tarts', and *Ochrolechia parella* has 'large pale grey sugar-dusted Bakewell tarts' which almost cover gravestones in many places.

The 'honey tarts' of the slightly scruffy Lecanora dispersa. *(Life size)*.

The small lichen *Candelariella vitellina* forms an irregular mustard-coloured crust, usually on the top of sandstone memorials or churchyard walls because it requires an acid substrate that is enriched with nitrogen. It is unusual in that it can survive in both polluted and unpolluted conditions and is common in churchyards, though sometimes overlooked because of its insignificant appearance. The yellow dye extracted from this lichen was used to colour the candles used in churches.

The moss, Pohlia nutans *(below), growing on a tree stump in Wales in April (Life size)*.

The lichen Cladonia fimbriata *(above), growing on a Welsh wall. (Life size)*.

There are several lichens which have a special connection with churchyards: *Caloplaca teicholyta*, white with a neat rosette, and *Candelariella medians* which resembles a scruffy golden-yellow *Caloplaca flavescens* (whereas *C. teicholyta* looks like a white version of it) seem to be more common there than elsewhere. The frond-like strands of *Ramalina lacera* are associated with the walls of ruined churches in the east of England. The ten or so known sites for the lichen *Lecanactis hemisphaerica* are mostly on ancient plaster-coated church walls, themselves rare, thanks to the Victorian passion for exposing walls, even ones which were originally designed to carry plaster. Another lichen, *Dirina massiliensis* f. *sorediata*, is native only on shaded cliffs in the north and west of Britain, but it has spread to churchyards and been observed in grey powdery sheets on hundreds of north-facing church walls in many parts.

It is rather more difficult to become acquainted with lichens than birds, or wild flowers, principally because there is no comparable range of field guides available. However, they are certainly one of the most important forms of wildlife that the churchyard shelters and there are many specialities of great interest in store for those who become competent lichen observers. The south-west holds such riches as *Ramalina, Evernia* and *Usnea* lichens, exotic in appearance with long branches, fronds and spidery hairs. In Norfolk the greenish *Haematomma ochroleucum* (so named because its fruiting bodies resemble bloodstains) and *Opegrapha saxatilis* are frequently discovered on north-facing church walls. Another *Opegrapha* is one of the few lichens that manages to grow on the acid, flaking bark of yew trees: *Opegrapha prosodea* is grey with spore-producing organs that look like small mouse droppings.

Occasionally lichen species are found growing an unexpectedly long way from their normal haunts. For instance, there is an attractive species which looks like a green map outlined and subdivided with black lines, called *Rhizocarpon geographicum*, which likes uplands and acid rock. I have seen it only high up on mountain boulders. How then does it come to be found in Monknash and St Bride's Major in Welsh lowland limestone country, or more perplexingly on a church roof in Norfolk? In the last case, the roof was of slate, and it has been suggested that the lichen may have survived, against all odds, from origins in an upland slate quarry.

A Ramalina *species of lichen, growing with* Lecanora *on the west wall of Meline church, Dyfed. (Life size).*

Not only the gravestones, but the graves and grave-mounds themselves provide an interesting micro-habitat for fauna and flora. Close-grazed or mown grave-mounds in chalky regions provide a habitat for attractive low-growing plants such as squinancywort, thymes and milkworts. Inside the kerbstones, grasses sometimes escape clipping, and larger kinds common in churchyards such as red fescue, tufted hair grass or its attractive cousin, wavy hair grass, can grow to their clumpy, mature form, and manage to flower and seed. Sometimes there are rarer grasses, such as the broad-leaved meadow grass, introduced in the eighteenth century and thriving in churchyards such as Lurgishall in West Sussex, Llangurig in Powys, and some others. The calcereous nature of many churchyards enables attractive chalk-loving species, such as quaking grass and yellow oat grass, to become established.

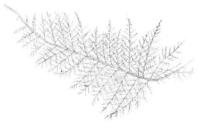

A filigree leaf of the moss Thuidium tamariscinum, *growing on damp ground in a shady corner.*

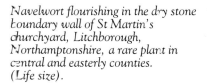

A moss (life size) in a ditch in Dyfed, identified as Dicranella heteromalla.

Navelwort flourishing in the dry stone boundary wall of St Martin's churchyard, Litchborough, Northamptonshire, a rare plant in central and easterly counties. (Life size).

93

Admirers of butterflies in the churchyard often forget that these beautiful creatures need a place to lay their eggs, and that the caterpillars need to feed, grow and pupate. Long grass in churchyards harbours many butterfly species in these stages of their life cycle. It also shelters some of the larger insects such as grasshoppers. I have seen dozens of meadow grasshoppers elbowing for space on the kerbs of a grave full of long grass.

Long grasses, on or beside graves, also provide shelter for the slow-worm, a species of lizard which was once very common in grassland, heaths and hedgebanks but now notably less so, having suffered, along with so many other creatures, from the destruction of its habitat. It is still, however, the most common reptile in Britain and the most regularly seen in churchyards. It does not bask in the sun as often as other reptiles, and is more often to be found beneath a flat sun-warmed stone or inside thick vegetation. Slow-worms have been known to survive for over fifty years, but they are by nature as by name, slow-moving creatures, and the speed and violence of rotary blades has dramatically reduced their numbers in churchyards.

Meadow grasshoppers in the churchyard of St Michael and All Angels, Cuxton, Kent, in early July, and common sorrel flowers whose arrow-shaped leaves taste like green apples. (Life size).

94

Coastal churchyards are probably the best in which to discover reptiles and amphibians, of which combined there are only twelve species native to Britain and a few introductions. I have been informed of numerous sightings of adders, common lizards and grass snakes sunning themselves on gravestones. Churchyards which have a damp area within them make a good habitat for frogs and common toads. Newts are also occasionally reported, not only the commonest British species, the smooth newt, but also crested and palmate newts.

Many native wild plants, though rare, occur in churchyards more frequently than might normally be expected and it is extremely difficult to discriminate between survivors of the native flora and planted specimens. I am fairly certain from the way in which it was growing that the double lady's smock growing in Bugbrooke churchyard in Northamptonshire had occurred naturally, but I could not give an opinion on the dozen or so others of which I was notified. This is a species which quite frequently throws up these delightful double-flowered forms in the wild. I have never seen or heard of the double lesser celandine in the wild, but it is a treasured cottage garden plant, and I believe originated as a natural 'sport'. There is only a single reported churchyard occurrence for this and for another intriguing 'flore pleno' form, the double wood anemone. A blue variant of the wood anemone is mentioned by the influential Victorian gardener William Robinson, and I recently found a description of it in a gardening handbook where it is named as 'Robinsoniana', but I have never seen it growing. The 'blue anemones' recorded in the churchyard surveys have so far turned out to be *Anemone apenina* and *Anemone blanda*, introduced garden species which have become naturalized from grave plantings.

Periwinkles (both lesser and greater) are frequently introduced to churchyards, and at St Mary's, Grendon, in Northamptonshire, there is an attractive double form of the lesser periwinkle with sky-blue flowers which I believe is the 'Azurea Flore Pleno'. The original 'Bowles' periwinkle with big deep blue flowers was actually found on a grave by the celebrated gardener Edward Bowles.

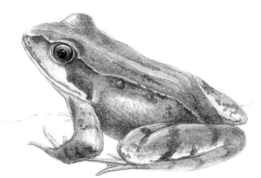

Common frog, no longer so common, in Syleham churchyard, Suffolk, which is by the River Waveney.

95

The double meadow saxifrage in the churchyard of St Nicholas, Worth, Sussex. The double flowers (drawn life size) are shaggy, and have pure white petals, flushed green-yellow at the centre.

The double meadow saxifrage, which was originally taken into cottage gardens from the wild, grows in very appealing abundance in the beautiful churchyard of St Nicholas at Worth in West Sussex. This is said to be the plant referred to in the nursery rhyme as 'pretty maids all in a row'. Some of the parishioners in Worth have attempted to grow it in their gardens, but it is believed to root only in the churchyard and so far at least, it seems none of them has met with any success.

I have been told that another old-fashioned double flower, the double soapwort, is to be found in the churchyard at Sutton in Suffolk and I have come across it myself, by chance, at St Michael's, Penbryn, in Ceredigion, Dyfed. This delightful churchyard overlooks woods, hills and sea cliffs, and when I visited it on a summer evening it was so still that I could hear the swish of the waves on the rocks far below. The churchyard was pleasantly overgrown, though it had been grazed (possibly by the sheep in the adjacent pasture), and rich in flowers. The carmine-pink double soapwort made a massive bouquet that completely filled one grave and was beginning to spread into the turf around it.

There was also at Penbryn the white form of the musk mallow, a plant which is found occasionally in the wild, sometimes in gardens and often in churchyards, although usually not in places where one might expect it to have been planted. As it grows well from seed, plants may perhaps have originated in grave bouquets, or arisen from earlier grave plantings that had disappeared. This interesting churchyard also held two kinds of toadflax—the pretty yellow sort, common and widespread, often found on graves and churchyard walls, and also pale toadflax, which is tall, with flowers a delicate lilac striped with darker purple, a native but not at all common plant.

The incidence of some of the scarcer native wild plants in churchyards can be a conundrum. It is not unlikely that snakeshead fritillaries might grow wild in churchyards. Old meadows which were incorporated into churchyards in order to extend their area during the nineteenth century might well have included fritillaries among their flora. They are, however, also treasured garden plants and out of the dozen fritillary churchyards I have been told about, at least one, at Lyndon in the Rutland district of Leicestershire, contains a known introduction. I have come to think that a blurring of origins is not a very serious matter.

Clustered leaves of double meadow saxifrage, growing low down in the moss-covered ground.

97

Snakeshead fritillaries at their best in early May in a Shropshire churchyard (life size). These were part of a sizable community which had been carefully mown around by those responsible for churchyard maintenance.

Snakeshead fritillaries are notoriously difficult to establish in gardens and are rare as wild plants. Where they have been successfully established in churchyards (and fritillaries have appeared at Lyndon every year since 1976), I believe that we should cherish them as much as the colonies we have in the wild. The phrase 'in the wild' requires a certain freedom of interpretation in the case of snakeshead fritillaries. These plants need to be kept in the manner to which they have been accustomed—the regime of the traditional water meadow—and are very vulnerable to changes in management. Nowadays, it entails a deliberate conservation strategy to keep in existence plants which thrived under an older system of agriculture. Places where fritillaries grow in any quantity are carefully managed by national or county conservation bodies.

Pygmy shrew just discernable among ferns in St Brynach's churchyard, Dyfed, in July.

The yellow star of Bethlehem which grows and seems to thrive in Kedington churchyard in Suffolk is another similar puzzle. I have always seen wild specimens of this plant growing by rivers, but at Kedington it is found, not by the river which runs along one side of the churchyard, but on higher ground. This species is said also to grow in damp pastures, but it is known only in three other sites in Suffolk (one, a small colony, has not flowered since 1937). It is a demure plant with a short flowering season. The yellow flowers do not appear every year, and the narrow leaves are often overlooked. It is not a plant one would expect to find planted in a churchyard, but possibly a botanically-minded vicar decided to experiment, or a parishioner heard of a colony that was about to be destroyed and re-planted it. The question remains open but meanwhile the healthy little colony continues to thrive.

In the churchyard at Scalby in North Yorkshire, there is rare native species called coralroot bittercress. I received word of it from a botanist who lives nearby and described the colony as a fine group of plants. That it is apparently well established is most surprising, since the species is a southern one, specific in its habitat and more or less confined to the Weald and the Chiltern Hills. No one has any idea how it came to be at Scalby.

Orchids are plants very vulnerable to any disturbance of their habitat or changes in its management. The overall population of orchids in Britain has declined dramatically over the past ten years, mainly because of changes in farming practice and land use. It is therefore cheering to find that about fifty surveys reported the presence of one or more species. The surprisingly large range of Orchid species recorded includes the greater butterfly orchid (Dyfed), the bird's nest orchid (Cumbria), and bee, heath-spotted, and southern marsh orchids at a number of sites. Some churchyards contain the orchids which are also to be found in the countryside around. In Jersey, autumn lady's tresses are present in almost every churchyard although they are rare on the mainland. The stately dark spikes of the early purple orchid are to be found both inside and outside churchyards in counties such as Devon and Sussex, as are twayblades and the bright pink triangles of pyramidal orchids in Suffolk. Common spotted orchids, which have a wide distribution, were also noted from churchyards in many counties (except those in the south-west, where they are less common).

In some counties, changes in land use have turned churchyards into a last refuge for certain species, such as the man orchid in Suffolk, where it is now very rare. In Surrey, the green-winged orchid is found in only a few localities, one of which is a cemetery, another a churchyard. This is an orchid which seems to be associated with churchyards in certain areas. I have seen specimens growing in several Sussex churchyards, surviving punishing mowing regimes. At Danehill, the mower had gone over just before the young spikes appeared and consequently the only plant species to be seen on the flat turf was the green-winged orchid. About a hundred small flowering spikes looked rather lost in their bare surroundings. There are also churchyard records from Hampshire and Suffolk, and I suspect that further research will show green-winged orchids to be present in churchyards in several other counties. They are a plant of meadows and pastures, a typical churchyard habitat. I heard a thrilling tale about this species which concerned a chapelyard in Ceredigion where green-winged orchids are not common. One spring when the regular mowing was interrupted, a host of a thousand or more green-winged orchids rose up out of the grass.

A robust green-winged orchid (life-size) in close-cropped grass in a Sussex churchyard. In meadow-like conditions, they can grow to more than twice this size. The flowers are purple with green-striped 'wings'.

101

One of the most interesting of the nationally rare plant species to survive in churchyards is the purple or yarrow broomrape, which comes up regularly in one of the coastal churchyards in north Norfolk. This broomrape is parasitic on the roots of yarrow, one of the commonest and most widespread churchyard plants. Also on record in churchyards are the fumitory, *Fumaria occidentalis*, which is found only in Cornwall, and its relative *Fumaria purpurea*, a plant which grows only in artificial habitats, and is endemic to Britain and Ireland.

Perhaps the most famous churchyard speciality is tall thrift, which grows not on sea coasts but inland, in dry lowland grass. It is taller than the common thrift and now survives in Britain only in a few meadows in the Ancaster valley (now a nature reserve) and in the extension to the churchyard of St Martin's at Ancaster, which is managed with conscientious respect for this rare species.

It is certain that as churchyards become more studied, several other nationally rare plants will be recorded. Apart from lichens, there are not many rare or threatened species which depend heavily upon churchyards, although a number of regionally scarce plants do. All plants have their own natural range, modified by the conditions of soil, habitat and climate, but they will sometimes grow 'out of bounds' in a favourable habitat. Some of the most characteristic churchyard species are rare in some parts of England and Wales, and in these localities are found only in churchyards. Hedge bedstraw and quaking grass, for example, generally scarce in the Ceredigion region of Dyfed, grow in some churchyards there. Similarly, in Jersey, so rich in flora that is rare on mainland Britain, hoary plantain is scarce, and churchyards are the most likely places to find it. The lichen *Candelariella medians*, though seen as a typical indicator of a lichen-rich churchyard in the south-east and eastern midlands, has its only known mid-Wales locality on the church door step at Llowes in Powys.

The bat population in Britain has been on the decline for many years, and despite the protection which is afforded in theory by the Wildlife and Countryside Act (1981), the analyzed figures of the Institute of Terrestrial Ecology's bat population survey, which began in 1978, show a continued decrease in numbers. There are great gaps in our knowledge of how bats live, but one of the main problems is undoubtedly the destruction of their

A handsome early purple orchid (life size), flowering in a Dyfed churchyard—one of the best sights of spring. The rector of this parish had actively resisted attempts to level the churchyard. The monstrous-looking black weevils are also painted life size.

103

habitat—there are now fewer places where bats can feed, roost, breed or hibernate. Among the remaining sites, churches and churchyards are crucial in terms of bat conservation. Bats have been seen in two-thirds of the Northamptonshire churches that are under observation by the county's Bat Group, and some of the most interesting bat roosts watched by the Durham Bat Group are in or near churches.

The emergence of the county Bat Group represents an exciting recent development in conservation. Bats are extremely difficult to observe, despite the fact that they live in close conjunction with human beings, often in artificial sites such as houses and churches, and our knowledge of them is scant. They are creatures of the twilight and night, both periods when human perception is at its least efficient. We cannot see them, most of us cannot hear them, and all of our senses are sleepy when those of bats are sharpest. However, Bat Groups are initiating a systematic observation of bats all over England, Wales and Scotland, sharing information and encouraging innovation in methods of study. Many half-truths once accepted as fact are being replaced by real information, and new questions are being formulated about bat behaviour.

A device which has helped observers to overcome some of the physical difficulties of bat watching is a 'bat detector' that makes audible the high-frequency echo-location calls made by flying bats. Groups are still learning to interpret the varied pips and squeaks from the little hand-held machine. Observers need to strain all their own senses, but working with the machine certainly does help in locating areas of bat activity and in identifying certain species, possibly high overhead, which might otherwise go entirely unnoticed. I would advise anyone interesting in seeing bats and who wishes to observe them locally, to go out first with a local Bat Group.

On my first outing in search of bats, I went with a group to a churchyard in the north of Buckinghamshire. The evening was still and warm. Pipistrelle bats were already flitting around between the church and the high trees of the churchyard when I arrived. Pipistrelles have a very characteristic flight, darting and fluttery, like that of a house martin. They

An evening sky filled with bat-wings over St Nicholas's churchyard, Brockenhurst, Hampshire.

are the most common British bats and the species most likely to be seen in churchyards. They roost socially, squeezed together in quite small crevices —in the Buckinghamshire churchyard, some had been seen tucked behind a false pillar in a high, west-facing statue niche, but they prefer a roof space just above the eaves, under hanging tiles or sometimes down behind the lead flashing where a church has been rebuilt and extended, between chancel and nave, for example.

Contrary to popular belief, belfries are not good places to find bats. They are far too full of dust and cobwebs; bats prefer a clean roosting place, and the sound of the bells would be intolerable for them. Church porches are another matter, although research in Northamptonshire suggests that bats avoid porches that are in use by birds. Out of two hundred and eighty-five porches surveyed by the Northamptonshire Bat Group, seventy-five were found to be occupied by pipistrelles, two by Natterer's bats, two by Daubenton's, two by long-eared bats and six by species so far unidentified. The bats usually roost between the underboarding and the roofing material, and most commonly used the part of the porch roof next to the church wall, which they reach by squeezing between the wall and roof timbers. Porches with plastered or stone ceilings are rarely used as roosts, since the bats are not able to find a point of entry into the roof space. Many church porches now have wire mesh gates to prevent birds—and bats—from entering. A sign on one church door in Northumberland is explicit: 'Please keep door shut and so help to keep out bats.' Nevertheless, nine Northamptonshire church porches equipped with wire mesh doors had confirmed bat roosts in them. It is always worth examining porches, even ones which at first appear unpropitious. Bats may use them as a way into the church, squeezing in above the church door, where there is often a gap—small scratch marks will show where they cling and scramble through. In the porch, a sharp-eyed observer may find bat droppings which resemble those of mice, but are dryer and more crumbly and have no smell. An expert in bat identification can tell different species from each other, on the evidence of their droppings.

Scarlet tiger moth (life size). Not widely distributed in Britain, this is a rare sight both in and outside churchyards—though it has been seen in several gardens around Oxford.

The presence of relatively fresh droppings indicates that a roost is in current use. We discovered new droppings from long-eared bats during my Buckinghamshire foray although we saw no long-eared bats at all that night. However, the moon was bright, and it is known that some insects, possibly including the noctuid moths which are among the long-eared bats' favourite prey, fly very high on moonlit nights. There were certainly records of long-eared bats on the site, but if they were flying high or deep within the tree canopy, we would not have been aware of them, since they do not register on a bat detector. Their huge, sensitive ears enable the bats to fix a position on the tiniest imaginable sounds, too high, not only for the human ear, but for the electronic ear too.

Just before dark, we saw a small bat clearly silhouetted against the sky, flying unwaveringly straight and quite slowly above our heads. It was a bat of the *Myotis* genus, and the visual evidence of its size, broadish wings and steady flight pattern, as well as its echo-location calls, confirmed that it was a Daubenton's bat. This species is to be found near still or slow-moving water, as it feeds by skimming insects such as caddis fly from the surface. It roosts, sometimes in churches, but also in large trees, such as willows, which may overhang the water. The attraction of this particular churchyard was the tributary of the Great Ouse bounding the southern

Insects (apart from butterflies) are an often overlooked component of the churchyard fauna. The random selection opposite represents only a small fraction observed in June and July. They are all drawn life size except the large striated capsid bug.

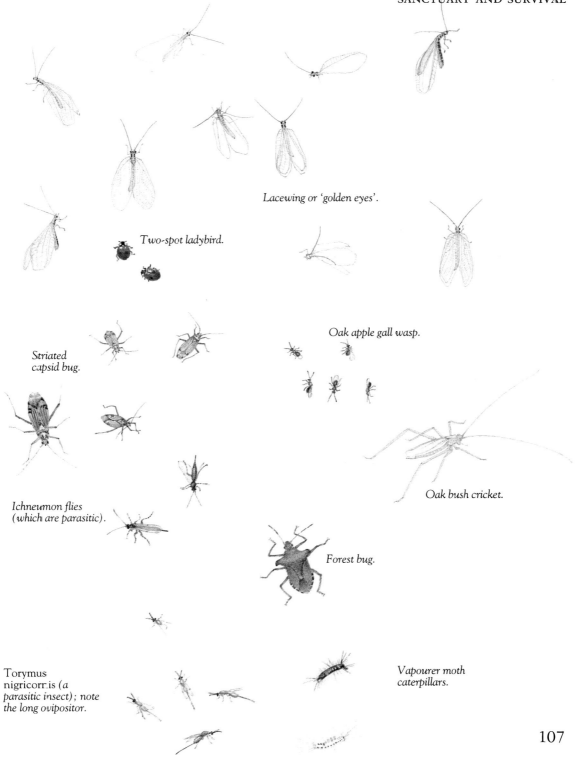

Lacewing or 'golden eyes'.

Two-spot ladybird.

Oak apple gall wasp.

Striated
capsid bug.

Oak bush cricket.

Ichneumon flies
(which are parasitic).

Forest bug.

Torymus
nigricorr.is (a
parasitic insect); note
the long ovipositor.

Vapourer moth
caterpillars.

107

edge. Later, when it was much darker, the Daubenton's sound came up again on the bat detector, as did that of another *Myotis* genus, the Natterer's bat, which we did not even glimpse.

As it grew late, we became aware of spasms of activity on the detector. They came and went too quickly to get a fix on them, but as we circled the church several times we caught the flash of a bat-wing in the moonlight and finally traced the apparent centre of activity to the south-east end of the chancel. Several times a bat flew close to our heads, and we eventually realized that there were two. A low-beam torch enabled us to examine the chancel wall just below the roof, where the small shape of a whiskered bat landed momentarily before darting off again. After a number of brief landings, the bat paused for a final moment, before disappearing swiftly into a crevice in the masonry beneath the end of the beam.

With its wings folded, the bat looked very tiny on the wide stone expanse of the church wall and, indeed, the whiskered bat is the smallest of the *Myotis* bats. A mature adult is only two inches in head and body length, although the wingspan can extend to about ten inches. This species is believed to inhabit English and Welsh counties northwards to Yorkshire, but it has recently been positively identified further north in a Northumberland church and vicarage. Whiskered bats use both buildings and trees for summer roosts and for hibernation. Natterer's bats will also use both but prefer very ancient churches which have become dilapidated enough to provide access through larger holes and gaps. They also show a preference for very mature trees, especially churchyard yews. Long-eared bats have a similar need for space, and will be found only in churches which have good-sized gaps in the fabric of the roof. They will colonize aisle roofs, if there is a generous space between roof and underboarding. The greater horseshoe bat, only occasionally found in churchyards, is restricted in distribution to south Wales and the south-west of England. This species is very sensitive to disturbance and chooses isolated, barely used or redundant churches. Almost opposite in its life-style and preferences is the noctule bat, which normally roosts and hibernates in trees, appearing less bothered by the presence of human beings in the vicinity. The noctule is sometimes found in suburban churchyards where there are large trees.

Acanthus (above and left), flourishing in the gardens of the churchyard of St James's, Piccadilly. There are several ferns and wild flowers in this churchyard, even though it is in the centre of London.

The desirability of a churchyard as a habitat for bats is influenced both by its vegetation and by the architecture of the church. Plant cover which provides plenty of insects, at least a few large trees, and a church built of soft stone such as limestone, rather than granite or other hard materials, make a generally favourable habitat, though each species has its own preferences. From a bat's point of view the peaks of church architecture are those periods, such as the Middle Ages, which produced a high level of elaborate stonework—pillars, arches, statues, niches, and other decoration. Tall trees and high hedges in the churchyard provide shelter as well as still pockets of air in which insects congregate. Insects are also drawn to a light by a lych-gate often left on throughout the night. Ivy attracts insects, particularly in early autumn, and young bats may feed around the ivy on large trees and churchyard walls, using its recesses as a temporary roost. Even in winter, bats frequent churchyards though the churches themselves show little sign of use. Some species use churchyard trees (especially hollow ones) for hibernation, and I have heard of their resting inside chest tombs during the early stages. There are a great many known reasons why churchyards are important to bats, and no doubt others will come to light as more is discovered about the life history of these little creatures.

Church porches are used for roosting and nesting by birds as well as bats (though apparently not at the same time) and many of the common churchyard species, such as house sparrows, blackbirds and starlings, readily colonize their beams and crevices. There are also numerous records of tawny and little owls, woodpigeons, and blue tits. Roofed lych-gates provide similar shelter. Swallows are often to be seen feeding in and over churchyards. Sometimes they breed there, though never in more than ones or twos, since even the porch and lych-gate combined offer little space for swallows, which are not strongly colonial. However, their nests are very much appreciated by other birds in following years. I was told of a porch in Dyfed where house martins took over the structures built by swallows and I have also heard of blackbirds building their nests on top of a kind of lid, which they made using the old swallows' nest as a bracket. Most exciting of all was a sight that I encountered on two occasions in Norfolk, where swallows' nests at the apex of a church doorway sheltered by a porch had been subsequently taken over by what I came to consider one of the most

Birthwort, a medicinal plant used in childbirth, is an introduced species. This rare plant is to be found growing in the grounds of several ancient monastic foundations and also, interestingly, in a few churchyards. This one was drawn (life size) from plants in a Suffolk churchyard.

characteristic churchyard birds, the spotted flycatcher. When I saw the first nest, the young had flown. The parents flitted around the churchyard, alighting on gravestones and executing complicated aerobatic figures as they caught insects which they took back to the fledglings waiting in the yew and pine trees. At South Pickenham I stopped, drawn to the attractive round tower rather than by any expectation of wildlife in a well-gardened churchyard. As I approached the porch I was greeted by the excited chirruping of nestlings which was hushed into silence only by stern calls from a parent flycatcher agitatedly perched on a nearby gravestone, its beak full of insects. But I caught a glimpse of a tiny feathered head peeping out of the nest in anticipation of its feed before they all subsided into the depths of their nest. This one, like the other, was a refurbished swallows' nest, built at the apex of the arch above the church door.

To birds and many other living creatures, mature trees represent more than a landscape feature: they are home and feeding place. However, big trees everywhere are being cut down faster than younger specimens are coming to maturity. Planting policies which ignore native species do

Rookery just outside the boundary of St. Bartholomew's, Warleggan, Cornwall, in mid-April, said to be the largest in the region. A Somerset name for the rook is 'church parson'.

nothing to help the situation. Churchyards, along with parks, both private and public, are becoming more important as habitat for those birds and other wild creatures that select tall trees as roosts, nesting sites or feeding places. Even with the large-scale disappearance of the elm, a tree popularly planted in the eighteenth and nineteenth centuries and splendidly full-grown in many churchyards until the ravages of Dutch elm disease, churchyards are still rich in fine, large trees, both native and exotic. Such mature trees provide a refuge for a number of bird species that are finding times increasingly hard.

The birds which have suffered most from the absence of elms are those familiar inhabitants of churchyards, the rooks. I was very pleased to hear their loud cawing in a good number of churchyards that I visited. There were rookeries in the churchyards themselves and often in adjacent gardens and parks. These birds have proved themselves adaptable since the disappearance of their favourite nesting places in the strong branches of elms. I have seen a rookery of up to fifty nests in horse chestnuts, another of about twenty in sycamores, and smaller colonies in beeches, willows, holm oaks and Monterey pines. The rook population of Britain has been declining for the last twenty-five years (that is since before the latest attack of Dutch elm disease), and tending towards smaller colonies. The days when hundreds of nests in a colony were commonplace are long past. It remains to be seen whether the rooks' breeding success in the alternative tree species is comparable with that provided by high, safe vantage points in the elms out of the way of most predators. Some of the new nesting sites—pollard willows for instance—are astonishingly low down for this species.

Although the provisions of the Wildlife and Countryside Act still allow for rooks to be shot all the year round by persons authorized by landowners to do so, they seem to live unharmed in churchyards and their environs. At Warleggan, a Cornish churchyard with a rookery adjacent to it, a local man remembered a time when the rooks were shot and seemed glad that this no longer occurred. Rooks have ecclesiastical associations: a Shropshire folk tale says that rooks do no work on Ascension Day, but sit quietly and reverently in the trees, and in the same county, according to the nineteenth-century expert on bird lore, the Revd Charles Swainson, it was thought that if you failed to honour Easter Sunday by wearing some new garment the rooks would 'spoil your clothes'.

Tall, old trees also offer shelter to woodpeckers, and all three species that breed in Britain are seen in churchyards. Once, when I stopped on impulse to investigate an agreeably overgrown town churchyard on the main road at Stourbridge, only ten miles or so from the centre of Birmingham, I disturbed a green woodpecker which had been unconcernedly catching ants on the grassy path, despite heavy traffic nearby. Making loud yaffle noises, it flew up into a large ash which stood between the churchyard and the adjacent school. I was again startled by that hard, laughing cry when another, very large and fine green woodpecker flew across my path as I was making my way up the drive to an out-of-the-way church in the Smethcott area, south of Shrewsbury. Then, only a few moments later, a buzzard flew across, so close that I could see every detail. I saw several buzzards floating over the churchyards in Shropshire and Wales, wings uptilted in typical languid manner. I have not seen them, but buzzards may well hunt in remote churchyards for larger insects, voles, mice and rabbits.

These small creatures also fall prey to owls, those birds so much associated with churchyards both in literature and in life. That most beautiful of birds, the barn owl, also goes by the name of church owl and in recent years this vernacular name has become truer in fact: in Suffolk and Norfolk, the only safe havens for barn owls are in isolated rural churchyards. Elsewhere too, changes in agricultural practice have reduced both food supply and nest sites, believed to be the main limiting factors on the barn owl population, which has now been declining for many years. In quiet rural churchyards there is a supply of food, and spires, towers and old trees with hollow places in which to roost and breed.

Tawny owls, larger birds which vastly outnumber barn owls, also nest in churchyards, principally in large trees in which there are holes, or in the disused nests of other large birds, and also in church towers. They take the same food as barn owls, including the odd sparrow plucked from a roost in ivy or elsewhere, but they tend to rely for a greater proportion of their diet upon earthworms and other invertebrates.

The best times to look out for the barn owl are at dusk or dawn, when it makes a splendid sight, beating like some wonderful ghost along a line of large churchyard trees. It is as well to be prepared for the strange unearthly shriek, which can be frightening in any surroundings, and not for those suffering from weak nerves or a romantic imagination. Anyone who cares about wildlife, however, will feel privileged to see this haunting bird. Tawny owls are much more readily heard and seen. I have listened to them hunting in and about my local churchyard until the early hours.

If you are lucky, you may see other crepuscular birds in certain parts of the country. At Minstead, in the New Forest, the hobbies which breed nearby come in over the churchyard trees or church buildings in swift aerobatic chase of small birds or the moths which also form part of their diet. To the same churchyard occasionally comes one of the most mysterious of all birds, the nightjar, a twilight creature strange enough even for Sir Arthur Conan Doyle, who is buried there. Its evening song, a low, continuous churring, carries for miles over the still forest after dusk, but it is not usually until the light has faded that the nightjar flies in search of noctuid moths and other large insects.

A spotted flycatcher, with a beakful of insects, uses a gravestone as a perch in St. Margaret's churchyard, Binsey, Oxfordshire, in early August. The green woodpecker (above) was sketched in St Mary's churchyard, Speen, Berkshire, in August.

115

In Devon, the black redstart has been seen in churchyards. Still a rare breeding bird in England, it is associated more with industrial rather than ecclesiastical architecture but it may be attracted by high ledges in ruinous churches. There are records of successful breeding in London churchyards and cemeteries. Another rare breeding bird, the crossbill, a colourful finch with a characteristic crossed-over bill in which the tips of the mandibles overlap, has been seen feeding in the large conifers of churchyards in East Anglia, but so far as is known has not yet made its nest in one. Spring (and in some years, autumn) may bring rare vagrants into churchyards. Several hoopoes have been recorded in southern counties, and a golden oriole rested briefly in the churchyard at Balcombe in Sussex.

Churchyards with an ample supply of berries are a focal point for a good many winter migrant birds, including some which are by no means common. Hardy churchyard observers who are prepared to visit during the winter as well as the summer have reported waxwings, which particularly enjoy rose-hips as well as haws and mistletoe, ivy and cotoneaster berries. During one winter, a nutcracker was seen in a Surrey churchyard.

Churchyards are used by almost every kind of bird which is to be seen in Britain—migrants, common resident species, even birds of specialist habitats, such as herons, seabirds, and waders. While churchyards cannot be considered crucial to their existence, there is no doubt that they are of significant benefit to a wide number of birds. Similarly for plants: a small proportion only of the total number of churchyards has received full botanical surveys, but even so, most of the plants on the British list have been found within them. Mammals from red squirrels to red deer, invertebrates from rather rare, pale, woodlice that inhabit the dark regions beneath grave urns, to the flamboyant dragonflies and humming-bird hawk moths, are seen in churchyards. There is hardly such a thing as a churchyard which is wholly devoid of interest to a naturalist, although sadly, less interesting, over-gardened ones have increased over the past few years.

A pair of kestrels nested in the church spire of St John the Evangelist, the Polish Roman Catholic Church in Putney, London, in early July. The family, including the two young, could be seen perching on the parapet together in the afternoons and evenings.

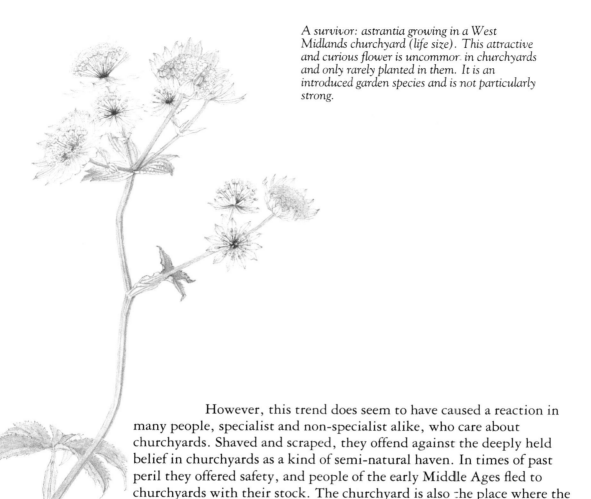

A survivor: astrantia growing in a West Midlands churchyard (life size). This attractive and curious flower is uncommon in churchyards and only rarely planted in them. It is an introduced garden species and is not particularly strong.

However, this trend does seem to have caused a reaction in many people, specialist and non-specialist alike, who care about churchyards. Shaved and scraped, they offend against the deeply held belief in churchyards as a kind of semi-natural haven. In times of past peril they offered safety, and people of the early Middle Ages fled to churchyards with their stock. The churchyard is also the place where the people of the parish install items of local, historical interest. At the church in Ivinghoe in Buckinghamshire, there is a great hook which was used to tear down the thatch from blazing buildings; coastal churchyards sometimes contain anchors or figure-heads, and many have village stocks re-erected in them. In Stanhope, once a thriving mining community in west Durham, a giant fossilized tree stump, thought to be over two hundred and fifty million years old, was removed to the churchyard where it now serves as a monument to the industrial past of this small town.

Conservation is second nature in churchyards, and in many places it already extends as much to the wildlife as to the ancient fabric of the church and the historical artefacts. Nature conservation in churchyards is a relatively new concept but it is one which most parishioners readily accept, probably because it fits so well with the traditional image. There is a considerable threat to wildlife all over Britain, much of it official and, as such, beyond local control. One is encouraged to think that the growing awareness of the role churchyards can play in conservation will mean that in many more places, plants and animals will find in them, a true sanctuary.

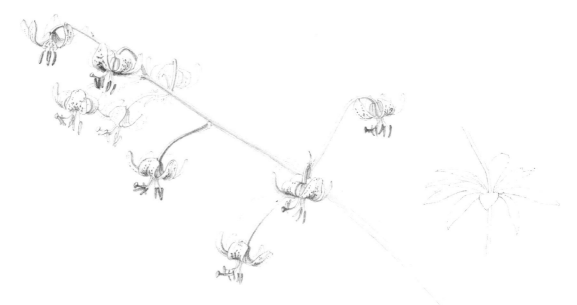

Martagon lily growing in the churchyard of St Mary, Ovington, Essex, in June. Other exotic lilies which have been recorded in churchyards are the tiger lily, Lilium pyrenaicum, Lilium regale, *and the Madonna lily which, because of its white purity, is the plant especially associated with the Virgin Mary and appears in countless paintings of her.*

CELEBRATION
and
CEREMONY

*O all ye Works of the Lord, bless ye the Lord: praise
    him, and magnify him for ever . . .
O ye Sun and Moon, bless ye the Lord: praise him, and
    magnify him for ever . . .
O ye Showers and Dew, bless ye the Lord:
O ye Winter and Summer, bless ye the Lord:
O ye Dews and Frosts, bless ye the Lord:
O ye Lightnings and Clouds, bless ye the Lord:
O let the Earth bless the Lord; yea, let it praise him,
    and magnify him for ever.
O all ye Green Things upon the Earth, bless ye the
    Lord:
O ye Wells, bless ye the Lord:
O all ye Fowls of the Air, bless ye the Lord:
O ye Servants of the Lord, bless ye the Lord: praise him
    and magnify him for ever.*

From the Benedicte

A PARISH CHURCHYARD IS NOT MERELY a piece of land surrounding the church. Even if it is not used as a burial ground it provides a place for remembrance, thanksgiving, and sometimes recreation. An awareness of its natural history often comes to people as an unexpected insight during some other activity. I was interested to find that it was not so much the isolated and neglected churchyards which were especially rich in wildlife, but often those which were the centre of a greater-than-average amount of parish activity in a town or village.

A wide range of secular events, as well as those connected with the church, takes place in churchyards. There may be craft fairs, flower festivals, strawberries-and-cream teas, markets, fêtes and even sports. There are nationally famous events such as the York mystery plays, and occasions such as local centenaries and anniversaries, which are important only to individual parishes. The celebration of baptism and marriage may include a procession or other traditional ritual in the churchyard, as the sombre ceremony of burial always does.

The calendar of the church itself has two great landmarks, Christmas and Easter, but numerous other minor and local occasions are traditionally observed in many parishes. A considerable proportion of all these churchyard events relate in some way to nature as does one of the best attended services of the church year, harvest festival. It is no accident that one of the most popular and well-known hymns is 'All things bright and beautiful'. A great deal of religious imagery draws on 'all creatures great and small'/'each tiny flower that opens, each little bird that sings'.

Churchgoers cannot fail to be aware of the links between religion and the natural world when the service of Morning Prayer (in all its forms) includes the poetry of the canticle, Benedicite, which is itself based on a more ancient hymn of praise, Psalm 148, with its splendid invocation of wild things and places.

The year in which this book was written was one in which the York mystery plays were performed. As in the fourteenth century, the performance still takes place out of doors in late June (around the feast of Corpus Christi) every fourth year. It no longer moves around the city, but is enacted in the ruins of St Mary's Abbey and its churchyard. The 1984 production brought

Ivy leaves (above) with the elongated central lobe typical of the common ivy, in St Mary's churchyard, Lower Heyford, Oxfordshire, in February. Holly leaves and berries (right), at All Saints, Fulham, London.

to the fore the authentic, unpolished voice of the original plays. It began, as the midsummer sun began to drop in the sky, with three plays concerning the creation of the world and all living things. Open-air theatre always has a special quality. When most of us spend the main part of our lives indoors, being out under the sky, in circumstances which are themselves memorable, gives us a heightened awareness of the world about us. We hear the evening song of birds; bats flit by as darkness falls; there is the constant accompaniment of wind and leaves, and the minute peripheral rustles and squeakings of night. After seeing the York plays, a friend of mine retained the memory of an additional drama — the shrieking and display of the peacocks. On another occasion, the barefoot apostles of one play only narrowly avoided a family of hedgehogs on a night-time excursion.

In the parish context, there are still places where local mystery plays and pageants are performed on a much smaller scale, regularly or on special anniversaries. At the church of St Nicholas in East Dereham, Norfolk, the play commemorates the miraculous event said to have occurred in a time of great famine in the seventh century, when deer came out of the forest in answer to Saint Withburga's prayer to the Virgin Mary. Their milk saved the starving people of the village. In 974, a rather discreditable plot resulted in the removal of Saint Withburga's body from East Dereham to the Cathedral at Ely, but a well with healing powers sprang up where her shrine had been.

As part of the anniversary service that I attended at East Dereham, the congregation walked in procession, singing, into the churchyard, where the holy well had been dressed with flowers and flower pictures depicting Saint Withburga and the Dereham deer. Planted around with honeysuckle, roses and herbs, the well was still brimming, even in a year of drought. House martins and swifts wheeled and fluttered above the churchyard. The light of the setting sun illuminated every separate feather of a sparrow's tail as it set down on a gravestone, and highlighted the robes of the priest and bishop as they bent to scoop up water from the holy well.

Flowers and greenery are still very much associated with church festivals, as they were in the past. Some of them are the traditional plants of the churchyard—holly, ivy, primroses, for example—others have become churchyard plants because they have been used in church decoration and seeded themselves when they were discarded: not only the garden form of gladdon called 'citrina', honesty, and lady's mantle, but more unusual species, such as *Kohlrauschia saxifraga*, which has a flower rather like a pink, and has been reported from two churchyards.

The plants most associated with Christmas are holly, ivy, and mistletoe, all of which grow in churchyards, though mistletoe, a plant sacred to the Druids, was never adopted into the Christian imagery and is rarely admitted into church. Holly, which figured in the celebration of the Roman feast of the Saturnalia, also has pagan associations, but is now so firmly established in the Christian tradition that it is referred to as 'Christmas' (though this name applies only to holly used as church decoration). In folk song and custom it is associated with the male principle, ivy with the female, a dichotomy exemplified in a fifteenth-century carol:

Holly and his mery men
They daunsen and they sing;
Ivy and her maidens
They wepen and they wring.

In the more modern Christmas carol 'The Holly and the Ivy', the holly provides the main theme and ivy is relegated to the refrain.

One of the principal church festivals celebrated by a procession before a service inside the church, is Palm Sunday. Since the true date palm of the Holy Land grows in Britain only as an introduced alien in the south-west (where it has been planted in a number of churchyards) the Church adopted other English plants to take the role of the palm fronds which were waved and strewn in the path of Christ on His triumphal entry into Jerusalem. The plant most often used is goat willow or sallow, also named pussy willow because of the soft furry catkins which appear in early spring; at this time, it is often called palm or palm willow. Yew is another plant which is sometimes carried on Palm Sunday and, in some northern counties, it, too, goes by the name of palm.

The Palm Sunday celebration is an elaborate presentation in some parishes. At Kirklington in North Yorkshire, the biblical scene is acted out by children in costume and the procession is led by a child on a donkey. Despite the capriciousness of early spring weather such pageantry is not exceptional, (though in one place the donkey proved too intractable and was dropped from the cast) but a more simple affair is more often the rule. At Kedington in Suffolk, the whole congregation assembles at a hut near the vicarage for a short sermon, then walks, singing, in procession along the road and through the churchyard into the church. Some people bring their 'palm' with them but, for those who do not, the vicar leaves a bucketful of willow palm at the start of the route and suggests that anyone who wishes might pull a branch from the vicarage garden or the churchyard as they pass, in the manner of the original Palm Sunday procession.

It used to be the custom in Wales to call Palm Sunday *Sul y Blodau* or Flowering Sunday. On that day, the graves were cleaned, trimmed and decorated with flowers and greenery. It seems that in earlier times, graves might have been dressed in this way on several occasions throughout the year. An account from Glamorgan mentions Easter, Whitsuntide and Christmas. It was perhaps a way of including the dead in the celebrations. However, by the end of the nineteenth century, the custom seems to have generally been confined to Palm Sunday. It still goes on in parts of Wales, but, although it has been recorded in the past in some Gloucestershire and Staffordshire villages, it never seems to have become widespread in England.

Umbels of ivy berries make decorative patterns on the churchyard wall, St Mary's, Lower Heyford, Oxfordshire. Once believed to ward off evil from domestic animals, ivy provides physical protection and food for a great number of wild creatures, from bats, birds and butterflies, to snails and small invertebrates.

125

A widely-observed activity is the making of 'Easter Gardens' during the days following Palm Sunday. They can be large, elaborate representations or homely, table-top scenes, but the elements always include the garden of Gethsemane, a hill topped by three crosses, and the tomb of Christ. They are made by local children out of moss, ferns, primroses and other decorative plants, which in many cases are picked from the churchyard or local woods.

It is interesting to see how churchyard ceremonies are hardly ever simple re-enactments of the past. They are adapted to suit the present-day needs and interests of parishioners. At Kedington, and in some other places, the old tradition of the Easter Hare who brings eggs has been revived in a Christian context. Easter eggs are hidden all over the churchyard, and after the Easter Sunday service the children in the congregation hunt for them.

Hymns and a Litany sung in procession through churchyard or fields, combined penitence with a supplication for God's blessing at Rogation tide (the week in which Ascension Day falls on the Thursday forty days after Easter Sunday). The official 'beating of the bounds' frequently took place at the same time. This practice reinforced in the collective parish memory the exact extent of the parish and is still observed in some places. At the church of St John the Baptist at Bisley in Surrey, a full beating of the bounds was made in 1983 to commemorate the seven-hundredth anniversary of the installation of the first rector of the church. Parishioners were spared from being dropped in streams and made to climb trees or stiles (as sometimes happened in the past), but they were 'bumped' against thirty-four local boundary landmarks. The ceremony took a whole day, beginning and ending in the churchyard.

Where the custom is preserved today, beating the bounds generally takes place only once every few years, and in a somewhat abbreviated form, though it usually begins or ends with a church service. A Rogation Sunday practice carried out in a group of four parishes near the Kent coast gives new meaning to an old custom. In the course of a walk over six-and-a-half miles, beginning after Holy Communion at St Oswald's, Paddlesworth, the participants go to St Mary and Ethelburga at Lyminge for Matins, to Postlin for Evensong and, finally, to Standford, where the day ends with Compline. Not all the parishioners walk the whole route, but the event is well supported even in bad weather and serves to draw the four parishes, each proud of its separate history and identity, into closer co-operation and friendship.

A prayer for God's blessing on the crops and natural bounty of a parish is still made in some places. At Lythe in North Yorkshire, the congregation walk singing to the fields and the sea. At Worth in Sussex, the vicar of St Nicholas leads the congregation up a lane and around the churchyard to ask for God's blessing on hedges, fields, crops and farm stock—a local farmer obligingly ensures that there are cows in a nearby meadow. If one is to judge from the churchyard and lane at Worth, brimming with wild flowers, ferns, birds and small animals, this is a method of churchyard management which should be taken up elsewhere!

Some country towns and villages persisted in their use of rushes or hay as a covering for church floors until the last century. The rushes, donated from every part of the parish, were renewed with great ceremony in late summer. A correspondent in Humberside described his grandfather's memory of the general excitement when the great rush cart, a hay wain piled high with rushes, 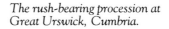 rumbled through each village.

The rush-bearing procession at Great Urswick, Cumbria.

127

Although there is no longer any need for such floor-covering, the rush-bearing ceremony is still observed in several English parishes. The two most famous rush festivals take place in Ambleside and Grasmere in Cumbria. In both cases, the rushes are carried in procession to the church where they are strewn and a service is held. A number of smaller parishes also observe the custom. At Barrowden in Leicestershire, the rushes are cut from church land on St Peter's Eve (June 28) and left to lie a week in the church. At the village of Great Urswick in Cumbria, rushes which grow around the tarn at the centre of the village are cut annually for the ceremony which is held on the church's patronal feast day at Michaelmas (September 29). The procession to the church is headed by a rush-bearing banner, and a traditional sheet, embroidered with rushes, is carried by four girls. Bystanders along the route place offerings for the church in the sheet. All the children carry flowers which they take out into the churchyard after the service, placing them on the oldest graves to show that the dead have not been forgotten.

At Glenfield in Leicestershire, new-mown hay is laid in the church in early July. In the church of St Peter and St Paul at Wingrave in Buckinghamshire, morris dancers or local children strew new-mown hay in commemoration of the bequest of a field to the church by a young woman who lost her way in the dark and was guided to safety by the sound of the church bells. At first, hay for the church was cut from the field, then the revenue from renting it out was used to buy floor-covering such as carpets and hassocks. The field was recently sold and the income put towards

The display of clipped yews in St Mary's churchyard, Painswick, Gloucestershire, consists of ninety-nine well-tended fastigiate trees.

maintaining the church floors. The celebration is now observed with hay donated by local farmers. (It used to be cut from the churchyard, too, but the grass is now mown too frequently to allow for hay-making.) At this time of year, Wingrave church and churchyard are the scene of special services, a fête, and surrounding the church with pennies—fifty pounds worth—in an atmosphere of holiday and general festivity.

Ringing the church with pennies (also carried out at Sutton in Cambridgeshire) seems to be a modern adaptation of the old 'clypping' ceremony, in which parishioners clypp (or clasp) the church, joining hands and walking round the building three times in a symbolic embrace. The meaning of clypping is sometimes misunderstood because the best known instance of it is at Painswick in Gloucestershire, also famous for its ninety-nine fastigiate yews, to which the clypping is mistakenly believed to refer. However, the service continues in many counties from Yorkshire (Guisley) to Cornwall (Helston), and it is being revived at Hastings in East Sussex and at Radley in Berkshire, where the clypping is followed by a sermon in the churchyard.

In medieval times, a considerable amount of money was raised for the church through public entertainment such as plays, dancing and fairs in the churchyard. These events were usually organized and often partly subsidized by the church. Churchwardens' accounts, rich sources of information, list items ranging from the erection of seating for a play, to fitting out morris dancers, and paying a child to dance the hobby horse.

Unnoticed for most of the year, the orb spider claims attention in the dewy days of autumn when its beautiful webs, spangled with droplets, sparkle from bushes and hedges.

Honeysuckle in St Brynach's churchyard,
Nevern, Dyfed, in mid-July. In some parts of
Britain, it was attributed with the power to fend
off evil from animals. (Life size).

130

There are signs that some churchyards are being reclaimed for a more general kind of community use. The Women's Institute survey disclosed a variety of parish events: church fêtes, fairs, sales of home produce, and—in the case of one woman who sits in the church porch selling bundles of lavender gathered from the churchyard of St Margaret's, at Cley next the Sea in Norfolk—churchyard produce.

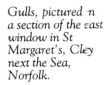

Major churchyard events usually take place in late summer, when mowing and trampling of the ground do no harm to the flora. On the contrary, it probably benefits. A well-attended late season fête has the same excellent effect as the practice of running cattle in a meadow; it keeps down the undergrowth and aids the dispersal of seeds—yellow rattle will not drop its seeds fully, unless subjected to this kind of treatment. At Roberttown in West Yorkshire, games held as part of the church fair take place on the north side of the churchyard where there are no graves. The widespread superstition that the north side of the churchyard was the province of the devil seems to have arisen during the Middle Ages. At St Michael the Archangel, Kirkby Malham, in North Yorkshire and St Nicholas, Worth, in West Sussex, the prejudice was strong enough to have caused the making of a 'devil's door' in the north wall of the church. The door was left open during a christening so that the devil could escape readily to his own plot. The Saxons appear to have been untouched by such fears—the best Saxon archaeological finds have been from excavations in the northern parts of churchyards, where the early graves have not been disturbed by later burials. Even today, the shaded northern plot is often the last to be filled and is still in many cases devoid of graves.

Gulls, pictured in a section of the east window in St Margaret's, Cley next the Sea, Norfolk.

Prolonged relief from soil disturbance in parts of the churchyard may be signalled by the presence of plants, such as orchids, which are particularly vulnerable to change. They are less likely to be found in areas used for burial where the ground may have been turned over to a depth of six feet or more several times through the centuries. Some grave-diggers restore the turf when they have filled in a grave, thus conserving all but the deep-rooted plants, but usually at least some of the soil gets inverted, in which case the less fertile soil from deeper down has to be recolonized and the result is likely to be a sward that is less rich than the original.

A Suffolk church mouse (house mouse to zoologists).

Lavender which grows (along with rue and rosemary) in the churchyard of St Margaret's, Cley next the Sea, Norfolk, is gathered (below right), made into bunches and offered for sale in the church porch.

The imagery of flowers is close to the heart of Christian liturgy. The burial service contains the idea that the life of a man or woman 'cometh up and is cut down like a flower'. Inherent in this, is the idea of resurrection. The dead will rise again as the wild flower on the grave reappears in springtime. Perhaps this is why flowers are so important in graveyard ritual and care, and why so many of us feel that the churchyard is a place for grasses and flowers.

The floral event that has caught the public imagination more than any other in recent years is the flower festival, which now has a firm place in many a parish calendar. Some flower festivals are publicized nationally. Held in the church and sometimes also in the churchyard, they give scope to the imagination for the expression of a renewed interest in flowers and, particularly, in flower arranging. In many cases, a flower festival is accompanied by other events such as concerts, as at Westleton in Suffolk, where the floral display consists entirely of wild flowers. At Needingworth in Cambridgeshire, the flower festival takes place at the same time as the well-dressing, and in other places it may be accompanied by craft stalls or tea for the visitors.

During my churchyard researches, I occasionally attended church festivals and special services, which stand out in my mind both as enjoyable and rather moving events. I had many agreeable and informative chance conversations with clergymen, vergers, churchwardens, gardeners, parishioners and other visitors, but it was when I was on my own among the plants, animals and gravestones, that I was most aware of the peaceful and comforting atmosphere which distinguishes churchyards from other places. I was therefore genuinely surprised when several people expressed the view that researching in churchyards was a morbid activity. In such pleasant surroundings it was easy to forget that churchyards also have a grim image, represented for example, in the terrifying scene which opens *Great Expectations* (thought to be based on Cooling churchyard in Kent), or the dour London churchyard which provides the background to the quarrel between Lizzie Hesketh and Bradley Headstone, or in innumerable horror stories. Such associations are part of our conception of churchyards, though by no means a dominant one; even in Bram Stoker's *Dracula*, it is acknowledged that 'the nicest spot in Whitby' is the parish churchyard which overlooks the bay, where 'there are walks, with seats beside them . . . and people go and sit there all day long looking at the beautiful view and enjoying the breeze.' Perhaps the most important feature about churchyards is that in them, one encounters death within a context of living things. For most people there is solace to be found in nature, and in the thought that the gravestones of those known and unknown to us have the society of birds and butterflies, lichens and wild flowers.

A dunnock built its nest behind this statue of St Andrew above the church door in Weybread, Suffolk.

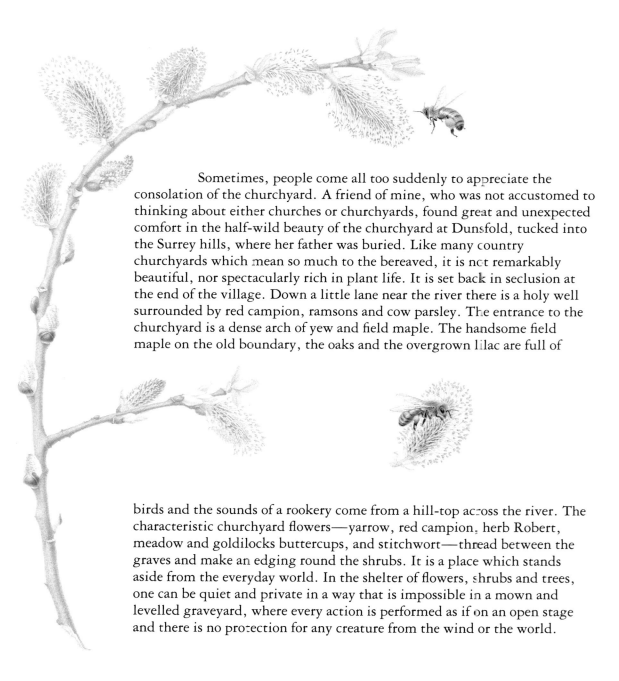

Sometimes, people come all too suddenly to appreciate the consolation of the churchyard. A friend of mine, who was not accustomed to thinking about either churches or churchyards, found great and unexpected comfort in the half-wild beauty of the churchyard at Dunsfold, tucked into the Surrey hills, where her father was buried. Like many country churchyards which mean so much to the bereaved, it is not remarkably beautiful, nor spectacularly rich in plant life. It is set back in seclusion at the end of the village. Down a little lane near the river there is a holy well surrounded by red campion, ramsons and cow parsley. The entrance to the churchyard is a dense arch of yew and field maple. The handsome field maple on the old boundary, the oaks and the overgrown lilac are full of

birds and the sounds of a rookery come from a hill-top across the river. The characteristic churchyard flowers—yarrow, red campion, herb Robert, meadow and goldilocks buttercups, and stitchwort—thread between the graves and make an edging round the shrubs. It is a place which stands aside from the everyday world. In the shelter of flowers, shrubs and trees, one can be quiet and private in a way that is impossible in a mown and levelled graveyard, where every action is performed as if on an open stage and there is no protection for any creature from the wind or the world.

Pussy willows like these seen in St Meubred's churchyard in Cardinham, Cornwall, in March, are carried in place of palms on Palm Sunday in many parishes.

The nineteenth-century poet and botanist John Leicester Warren, Lord de Tabley, was neither the first nor the last to gain strength in bereavement from the beauty of a churchyard and its wild plants and birds. He wrote in 'The Churchyard on the Sands':

> The grey gull flaps the written stones,
> The ox-birds chase the tide;
> And near that narrow field of bones
> Great ships at anchor ride

> A church of silent weathered looks
> A breezy reddish tower,
> A yard whose mounded resting-nooks
> Are tinged with sorrel flower

He notes the succession of churchyard flowers and birds:

> Let snowdrops early in the year
> Droop o'er her silent breast;
> And bid the later cowslip rear
> The amber of its crest.

> Come hither linnets tufted-red,
> Drift by, O wailing tern;
> Set pure vale lilies at her head,
> At her feet lady fern.

> Grow samphire on the tidal brink,
> Wave pansies of the shore
> To whisper how alone I think
> Of her for evermore.

> Bring blue sea-hollies thorny, keen,
> Long lavender in flower;
> Grey wormwood like a hoary queen
> Staunch mullein like a tower.

Swallows congregate over St Mary's churchyard, Swinbrook, Oxfordshire.

Old-fashioned churchyards are, by their nature, places of seclusion and shelter not only for the bereaved but for any visitor. Such surroundings, old tombs and headstones, sheltered by overgrown box or yew, make a good place to resolve troubled thoughts or simply to sit quietly.

Even when it was customary for people of status to be buried inside the church, there were those who chose the churchyard for their eventual resting place. In a letter written to Matthew Smith in 1750, Edmund Burke wrote that he 'would rather sleep in the southern corner of a little country churchyard than in the tomb of the Capulets'. (This seems to have been a rhetorical desire, however, for he was buried inside the parish church at Beaconsfield, apparently according to his own wish.) Another who expressed his desire to be buried out of doors, though as a clergyman he would have been entitled to intramural burial, was the metaphysical poet Henry Vaughan, whose grave is at the foot of a yew tree in Llansantffraed churchyard, overlooking the River Usk, which provided the inspiration for so much of his poetry. Nicholas Ferrar, the seventeenth-century religious aesthete, was precise in his instructions that he should be buried seven feet from the west door of the church at Little Gidding in Cambridgeshire, where his tomb can still be seen. It is now situated a little further from the church, which has been foreshortened since Ferrar's death, probably during the Restoration. The path by the pigsty mentioned by T.S. Eliot in *Four Quartets* has recently been re-routed and the sty itself converted, but the small churchyard, despite being kept monotonously neat, is still a pleasant place, full of bird-song from the hedge and sycamore thicket which surrounds it. Caradoc Evans, known for his Anglo-Welsh short stories, wrote the inscription for his own grave at Horeb Chapel, New Cross, in Ceredigion. His stone, dated 1945, reads: 'Bury me lightly so that the small rain may reach my face and the fluttering of the butterfly shall not escape my ear.' The chapelyard is still flowery and full of butterflies.

It is evident that well before the time of Thomas Gray, churchyards were regarded as beautiful and exceptional places, but it was the 'Elegy Written in a Country Church Yard' which not only incorporated those sensibilities of the past, but provided an image of them, so powerful that it has coloured our perception to this day. Above all, this poem firmly established a sense of the churchyard as a special kind of English landscape. It certainly had an influence on the idea of what a churchyard should look like, confirming their rural qualities. This ideal of the country churchyard is still, more than two centuries after the poem was published, the most important factor in our attitude to them.

Gray himself spent much of his later life studying botany and achieved some eminence in the subject. The 'Elegy' does not burst at the seams with natural history as became the fashion in a later period; his ideals were conciseness and perspicuity. Although some of the elements in the 'Elegy'—'the ivy-mantled tower', moping owl, and rugged elms, were familiar poetic territory in the eighteenth century, one has the impression that the stock imagery conformed to his observations, not the other way about. Other details: the lowing herd and the ploughman, the cock crow, the beetle's droning flight and the twittering swallow, summon the scene recognizably, even now.

In the original version of the 'Elegy' (and printed in some of the first editions) were four more lines, of naturalistic detail, just before the Epitaph. Gray apparently decided to omit them later, on the grounds that they made too long a parenthesis at this place in the poem.

> There scatter'd oft, the earliest of the year,
> By hands unseen are show'r of violets found;
> The redbreast loves to build and warble there,
> And little footsteps lightly print the ground.

Haymaking in progress (left) in August in St Nicholas's churchyard, Oakley, Suffolk.

137

Gray foresaw that the 'Elegy' would be a success; he drew attention, in a letter, to how popular Edward Young's 'Night Thoughts' and Hervey's 'Meditations on Tombs' had been just before his own poem was published. Gray could not have known, however, how profoundly people would take the 'Elegy' to their hearts. It has been taught to generations of schoolchildren, some at least of whom were told, unequivocally, that it was the best poem in the English language. Even today, people who know no other poetry can recite Gray's 'Elegy'.

Many poets since Gray have written about churchyards. Their work is in the English pastoral tradition, poems which see the churchyard as enshrining the best country idylls, shelter and peace. 'The winds were still' wrote Shelley—a notable atheist—of Lechlade churchyard, 'or the dry church tower grass,/Knows not their gentle motions as they pass.' Wordsworth describing a 'Churchyard among the mountains' in 'The Excursion' also looked at it as a special kind of grassland:

> Green is the Churchyard, beautiful and green
> Ridge rising gently by the side of ridge,
> A heaving surface, almost wholly free
> From interruption of sepulchral stones,
> And mantled o'er with aboriginal turf
> And everlasting flowers.

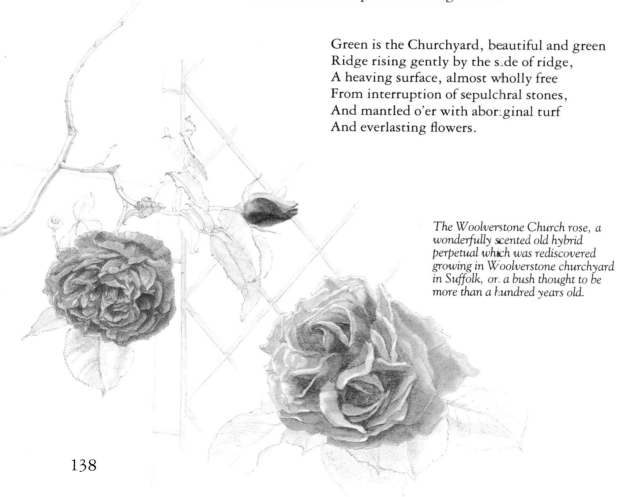

The Woolverstone Church rose, a wonderfully scented old hybrid perpetual which was rediscovered growing in Woolverstone churchyard in Suffolk, on a bush thought to be more than a hundred years old.

The parson-poet and botanist Andrew Young wrote lovingly of the little
east Suffolk church at Friston, and how in Church Field 'the scented orchis/
Shoots from the grass in rosy spire . . .'

Sir John Betjeman was, more than any other, the poet of English
churches and churchyards. In a light-hearted poem about St Enodoc in
Trebetherick, north Cornwall, where now he is buried, he wrote of going to
this most extraordinary ancient church with its strange uneven spire, which
stands just clear of the sand that once buried it.

> Come on! come on! This hillock hides the spire,
> Now that one and now none. As winds about
> The burnished path through lady's finger, thyme
> And bright varieties of saxifrage,
> So grows the tinny tenor faint or loud
> And all things draw towards St. Enodoc

> . . . . Hover-flies remain
> More than a moment on a ragwort bunch,
> And people's passing shadows don't disturb
> Red Admirals basking with their wings apart.

As the clergyman addresses the congregation inside
the church:

> "Dearly beloved . . ." and a bumble-bee
> Zooms itself free into the churchyard sun
> And so my thoughts this happy Sabbathtide.

['*Sunday Afternoon Service in St. Enodoc Church, Cornwall*']

The interests of churchgoers, mourners and naturalists need not be at odds.
The church sits within an island of natural life, and there is a sense of its
presence at St Enodoc as thoughts wander with the bee, or, on another
occasion, in the church of St Nicholas at East Dereham, when the great west
doors open to the red-gold sun of midsummer evening and to the
background of the quiet Norfolk landscape veiled in haze.

*This rose (above) was planted on the grave of
Edward Fitzgerald in St Michael's churchyard in
Boulge, Suffolk, in 1893. It had been raised in
Kew Gardens from seed brought by William
Simpson, artist-traveller, from the grave of
Omar Khayyam at Naishapur, and planted by
admirers of Fitzgerald in the name of the Omar
Khayyam Club.*

139

In almost every aspect of the furnishing and decoration of the church one can find reflections of the natural life outside. Sometimes they are explicit and local, as at the church of St Petrock at Lydford in Devon, where the Revd G.S. Thorpe was inspired, it is said, during a thunderstorm, to take the Benedicite as the theme for carvings on the pew ends. There we find fine representations of the animals and plants to be found in a Devon churchyard and the surrounding countryside: a thrush with snails, a sparrow on its nest, a woodpecker, daffodils, violets, foxgloves, wood anemones and ferns. There is oak foliage with acorns, a field maple, and a beech tree with a squirrel in it. There is even an adder.

Similarly, at the church of St Mary at Swaffham Prior, Cambridgeshire, there is a large window of pale, watery blue and green stained glass representing the Benedicite. The water lily, sagittaria and bullrush are plainly recognizable, as is their marshland habitat which is one of the last fen sites—Wicken Fen, a property of the National Trust since early last century, and now a nature reserve.

Topiary bird of golden yew, at St Margaret's, Alstone, Gloucestershire.

140

The natural life of the churchyard and beyond finds expression in the fabric and ornamentation of the church, as it has in the liturgy itself. On the outside of churches, animals and flowers are represented in the stonework, often most memorably as gargoyles. Many of the creatures depicted in gargoyles are fantastic and nightmarish, but others, such as the hare and hound on the church at Kilpeck in Herefordshire, are realistically portrayed.

Some fine, naturalistic weathervanes swing in the wind above parish churches. Most are cockerels, but variations include a fine salmon at Upper Framilode on the Severn, to the south-west of Gloucester and, with equal local relevance, a mallard in flight on the timber bell tower overlooking Walland Marsh, just below Romney Marsh, where the wild duck are as integral to the landscape now as they were in the late eightenth century when the weathervane was made. But nature is not to be outdone. Both cormorant and shag have been observed perching on the weathercock of Norwich Cathedral spire.

Exterior church carvings from St Mary's, Speen, Berkshire (above) and St Mary's, Brome, Suffolk. The cat-faced gargoyle (top left), also on Brome church, provides an unusual site for a bird's nest.

141

Owls are a favourite subject among the carvings to be found on misericords because, it is said, of the prophecy in Isaiah (chapter 12. v21) that when Babylon is destroyed, its houses will be tenanted by 'doleful creatures; and owls shall dwell there' (though some translations obscurely substitute ostriches for owls). Just as certain saints are brought in to illustrate a local point, Isaiah may well provide a useful route by which to introduce familiar birds of the churchyard and country into church decoration. Other misericord subjects are oak woods with pigs rooting for acorns, fox and hounds, hare and hounds, and roses. At the church of Edlesborough in Buckinghamshire, rightly esteemed for its wood carving and set in one of my favourite churchyards, the misericords depict not only owls but also the very much more unusual subject of bats.

Ivy berries mature from yellow-green to green-black. They are a favourite with overwintering blackcaps.

The naturalistic stone carvings at the chapter house at Southwell Minster in Nottinghamshire are justly famous. There, thirteenth-century masons coaxed the stone of the capitals and vaulted roof into a tumble of foliage 'which is as luxuriant as the undergrowth of a hedgerow in May when subjected to wind and rain', as E.H. Crossley, a connoisseur of church craftsmanship, described it. The plants are so naturalistically depicted, and with such skill, that one can identify holly and ivy, hawthorn with berries,

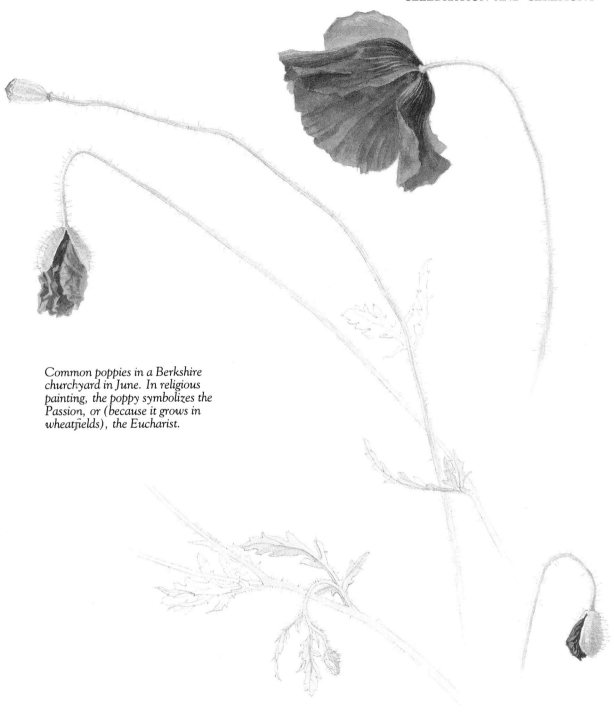

Common poppies in a Berkshire
churchyard in June. In religious
painting, the poppy symbolizes the
Passion, or (because it grows in
wheatfields), the Eucharist.

143

and both the native English species of oak. There is also, I believe, sycamore, one of only two such early church carvings that I know—the other is at Christchurch Cathedral, Oxford. The sycamore's wide-lobed leaf and paired seeds, joined in a narrow angle, are quite distinct from those of the field maple, which is also to be seen at Southwell. The field maple has smaller leaves with more rounded lobes, the angle of its seeds being so wide as to set them almost in a straight line. The Southwell carvings also depict other plants of the countryside, and indeed of the churchyard: buttercups, white bryony, hops, vines and roses. Professor Nikolaus Pevsner, whose masterly description of *The Leaves of Southwell* has brought these beautiful carvings a wider appreciation, remarks that the roses are a double form and not, as most of the other foliage, a wild variety that might be expected in the hedgerow. I note, in passing, that I have seen many double roses of this kind in churchyards. Whether they were there in the thirteenth century, it is impossible to say, but the most popular medieval poem of all, *The Romaunt of the Rose* (by Guillaume de Lorris and Jean le Meung) was written not long after the leaves were carved. The rose figures in monastery gardens and was used for garlands in church processions. For Pevsner, the leaves of Southwell represent an artistic achievement that is firmly rooted in the context of freer and more imaginative religious and philosophical attitudes which developed in the early thirteenth century and reflected an increased awareness of nature itself.

> Could these leaves of the English countryside, with all their freshness, move us so deeply if they were not carved in that spirit which filled the saints and poets and thinkers of the thirteenth century, the spirit of religious respect for the loveliness of created nature?

[*Sir Nikolaus Pevsner: The Leaves of Southwell*]

A great deal of that feeling for nature is still manifest in parish churches. It no longer shows itself in great works of building. The religious energy for building and rebuilding churches is no longer there and perhaps, in any case, we have grown to love our old churches too much to want to change them. What is remarkable, in an age whose interpretative models of the world are almost entirely mechanistic, is the way in which natural images

A coal tit, a bird associated with churchyard yews and false-cypresses, at St Andrew's, Winston, Suffolk.

continue to prevail in church decoration. Flowers and animals feature in items bought or made professionally, such as stained glass, carpets and woodwork. They are even more common in things made for the church by parishioners themselves: the tapestry hassocks, banners, beautiful flower-embroidered altar cloths, even a rug before the altar at Long Compton in Warwickshire, composed of panels depicting wild and garden flowers.

Sometimes the plants of an individual churchyard are mirrored inside the church. At St Peter's, Theberton, in Suffolk, a modern wrought iron communion rail with ivy foliage in the decoration echoes the luxuriant growth of ivy over the tombs outside. The choir stall beyond has carved oak foliage and acorns, in harmony with an overgrown part of the churchyard behind the church which is almost an oak thicket. Memorials inside the church, which tend to be grander than those outside, are generally restricted to classical subjects, and naturalistic detail is mainly confined to cornucopia spilling over with fruit, flowers and ears of grain (reflecting a rich life), willows (for grief) and formal garlands.

A common garden snail half-hidden by ivy on the church wall, at Cilgwyn Dyfed, in July. (Life size).

Common reeds (Phragmites) are picked from the tarn in the village of Great Urswick, Cumbria, to be carried by the Rush Queen in procession during the annual rush-bearing ceremony.

These subjects also appear on the gravestones and memorials in the churchyard, which have a wider range both of the choice of theme and in the quality of the workmanship than interior carvings. The early nineteenth-century work in particular shows a freedom and creativity of expression in gravestones which feature well-observed animals such as sheep or pheasants, occasionally butterflies (signifying the soul), and individual plants including honeysuckle, bryony, roses and ears of wheat. Some gravestones depict cut flowers, roses, violets or lilies, or blooms with severed stems, which signify early death. Later in the century, grave-carving became more conventional; the imagery and its style of execution were standardized—ivy, lilies, forget-me-nots and doves monopolized the gravestones. However, in the context of a country churchyard, even

quite ordinary gravestones standing among wild flowers and trees have their charm. In the isolated churchyard at Drayton Beauchamp in Buckinghamshire, a plain grave is transformed in appearance by a dense velvety pool of dark green lesser celandine leaves growing within the rectangle of the kerbstones. The only nearby building is the rectory where the botanist Henry Harpur Crewe once lived. There is no trace now of his famous pink snowdrops but there are places which are white with the more familiar kind. Beneath a bank by the boundary of the churchyard, there is a grave all overgrown with ivy, single and double snowdrops and winter aconites. The ivy on the ground perfectly sets off the brightness of the flowers, and two or three strands climb up the stone grave cross, their starry leaves mingling with those of the stone-carved ivy.

147

COMMUNITY
and
CONSERVATION

He passes down the churchyard track
On his way to toll the bell;
And stops, and looks at the graves around,
And notes each finished and greening mound
Complacently,
As their shaper he,
And one who can do it well . . .

Thomas Hardy: *The Sexton at Longpuddle*

THE PARISH CHURCH IS USUALLY THE main landmark of a village and, despite urban development, an important feature in the town landscape. Old churches and churchyards have for a long time been a focus for students of history and architecture. More recently, archaeologists and naturalists have begun to devote serious attention to them. It is easy however, for scholars and enthusiasts to concentrate on details of their subject and to forget that the churchyard still has a practical function, and a role to play in the community life of the district. Any ideas about wildlife conservation need to take into account the feelings and needs of the people of the parish or they are probably impossible to put into practice. If directions for churchyard management come from the outside they can readily stir up resentment, and it is all too easy for an adviser to trespass unwittingly on private feelings about particular parts of a churchyard.

Churchyards develop their own internal logic. Pathways are made or disappear depending on which parts are used for burial. Tragedy, inevitably bound into the history of every churchyard, reveals itself in the paths trodden by the bereaved. There is a new path through tall wild flowers and grasses in a Hertfordshire churchyard that I know well, which was worn by the constant visits of the bereaved parents to the grave of their young child. After a few months, the parishioner responsible for the churchyard grass adopted the track into his regular round of mowing, bringing it into the semi-formal network of pathways, and providing a route for other mourners and visitors to a previously inaccessible part of the churchyard.

The wildlife of the churchyard adapts to the changing patterns of use. The grass around new graves is, by common consent, usually kept short, but that surrounding older, less visited ones, may gradually be mowed less frequently. The area in which the oldest graves are located is probably the quietest and least disturbed and often shelters high numbers of birds, small mammals and insects in well-grown shrubs and taller grass.

There does not need to be a defined management policy for a churchyard to be well cared for. In many parishes, the feeling for nature conservation, if not explicit, is evident in the care with which the churchyard is looked after. Sometimes it is a special contact with living things which has created an awareness of the wildlife of the churchyard and a desire to conserve it. Such a revelation occurred at a spring wedding in a Northamptonshire village. No-one present could have failed to take

*Flat-backed millipede (left)
with detail of body segments,
and centipede (below).
(Both life size).*

150

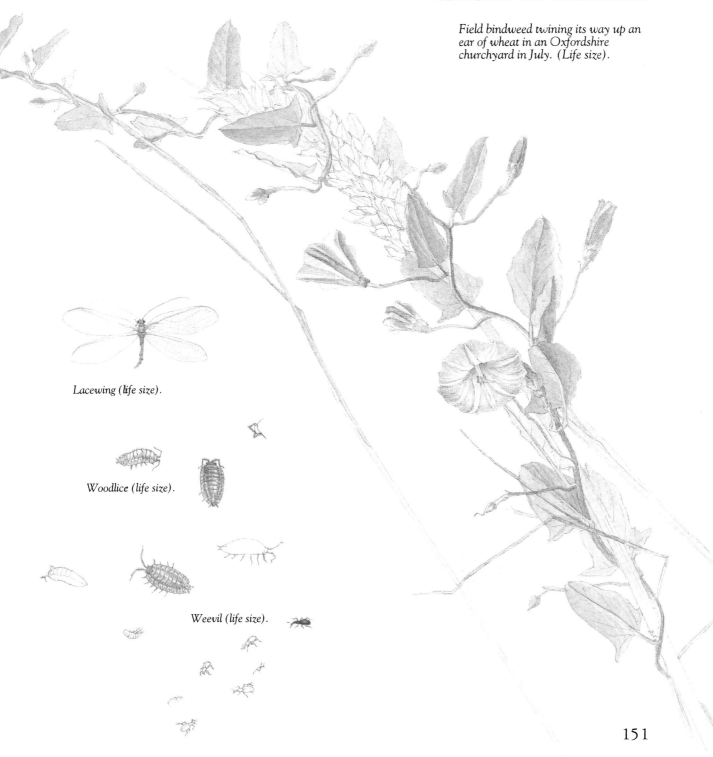

Field bindweed twining its way up an ear of wheat in an Oxfordshire churchyard in July. (Life size).

Lacewing (life size).

Woodlice (life size).

Weevil (life size).

151

pleasure in the harmonious picture of the bride and bridesmaids in their chosen colour scheme of blue and pale yellow seen among bluebells and primroses. It is still talked about, and photographs are shown to visitors. Should there be any scheme to close-mow that particular churchyard, there will be many voices of dissent.

A positive attitude towards conservation is likely to arise when there is an intimate and sustained experience of a churchyard and the wildlife in it. An excellent example of happy co-existence between humans and wildlife is to be found in the churchyard in Ripponden in West Yorkshire. The local playgroup uses an open space in the churchyard for its activities when the weather is good. On a May morning when I was there, the young children were all out on miniature bikes and cars, in their little playground on the west side of the church, while the churchyard gardener began to cut back the high sweet cicely and long grass nearby, and a dipper flew swiftly along the river which formed one boundary to disappear into a culvert in the bank, where, doubtless, it had its nest. There was also a grey wagtail on the river, flashing bright yellow as it bobbed about. All along the riverside sweet cicely was in flower, but on the opposite side of the churchyard, rhododendron and massed bluebells were dominant, and the pretty pink purslane speckled the bank. Nearer to the church, the shorter grass was full of daisies. Sweet woodruff and some London pride had spread from the graves to colonize the grass round about them. Tall, elegant fern fronds between the graves swayed in the breeze. At the very least, those small children would learn that churchyards are beautiful, peaceful places. It is likely that incidentally, they were also learning quite a lot about nature.

There are many schools, originally church foundations, built beside churches with independent access to the churchyard. Some have their own gate, but the welcoming churchyard of St John the Baptist in Glastonbury also has a special paved path leading from the school across the churchyard to the church. Adults, as well as children, come to this churchyard in summer to have a packed lunch or simply to sit in the sun enjoying the scent of the wallflowers. The Victorians used to make

English partridge seen under the hedge in Holy Trinity churchyard, Boxted, Suffolk, in April.

an outing of a picnic in a churchyard, but nowadays this habit seems to be confined to churchyards in town centres, although there is a parish picnic at St Peter's, Tadley, in Hampshire on the Sunday before St Peter's Day.

Children make unofficial use of the churchyard too and I often came across small groups of them playing among the shrubs and gravestones. One churchyard naturalist confided in an unguarded moment that children are a good indicator species—where they choose to play, the churchyard is likely to be rich in wildlife. Not everyone would agree: a vicar in West Yorkshire recently made a special plea to his parishioners not to allow their children to play in the churchyard. Yet, surely, children are more likely to grow to appreciate and respect the churchyard by being in it than from being kept out?

A considerable degree of practical conservation is inspired from within the parish. The results may not be as extensive as a naturalist might wish, but such care usually has the advantage of being sustained over a long period. Churchyards have to fulfil so many expectations that it would be foolish for anyone to try to establish a kind of model to which they should all conform. Indeed, if churchyards were all turned into standardized nature reserves, we should lose a lot of the excitement and unpredictable variety which occurs in places where human activity and wildlife are in close proximity. We should also lose the results of churchyard grave-planting, which has been continuous over centuries and displays itself in the diversity of naturalized flora and unusual trees.

Oxford ragwort flowers and full and empty seed heads, seen in June (life size). Note that the bracts on the flowerheads are all black-tipped.

153

Yet there are dangers in being too sanguine. When we assume that the churchyards muddle along all right, we would do well to remember that the churchyard at Kettlewell in North Yorkshire used to have lady's slipper orchid (for which there is now only one known site in Britain), and that within living memory there were natterjack toads in Norfolk churchyards. It is also true that careless repointing and restoration have obliterated many historic and botanically important sites for ferns. On the other hand, one should not underestimate the problems encountered in seeing that the churchyard is maintained at all. Many incumbents of rural 'group practice' churches are at their wit's end, when faced with the apparently boundless fecundity of a country churchyard.

Unfortunately the methods used to restore order are often too drastic and destructive. Though I have often heard it categorized as such, these actions are rarely deliberate vandalism, rather that people fail to consider wildlife because they associate it with an unkempt, overgrown environment, not at all suitable for a consecrated burial ground.

It cannot be emphasized enough that wildlife conservation in a churchyard does not mean a churchyard wilderness. Indeed, an overgrown habitat is inimical to many of the characteristic churchyard species. Not a great deal of labour is required to maintain a churchyard which is neat but which shows a concern for its natural life and which is a rewarding place by any standards. It need not necessarily be one that contains great rarities, but simply one in which a naturally beautiful setting is cared for with sensitivity for the landscape, and the plants and animals within it. There are still many such churchyards to show us example.

At Sourton in Devon, the churchyard backs onto a disused railway line which in its working days carried the seeds of pink purslane up to the boundary hedge of the churchyard, where it has outlived the railway. Jackdaws nest in the tower, goldfinches use the pollard sycamores as singing posts, and a willow warbler trills from a tall hawthorn up the hill. Further into the south-west, the church of St Symphorian sits at the heart of the Cornish village of Veryan, with a holy well opposite the gates. In the sheltered mildness of the churchyard grow high beeches, with ramsons lush beneath, and masses of three-cornered leek (which looks slightly like a white bluebell from a distance). There is a rookery in the pine trees, and the camellias lining the path to the church porch flourish in this gentle climate.

Pale flax, a wild plant found in many
coastal churchyards, here growing in
the chancel of a ruined church, high on
the cliffs at Rufus Castle, Portland,
Dorset, in June. (Life size).

Field forget-me-not, growing with the
flax in St Andrew's, Rufus Castle (life
size). This is the most common of the
churchyard forget-me-nots.

155

Any visitor, botanist or not, could spend happy hours enjoying the glorious limestone flora of the Dales in churchyards such as St Mary's, Kettlewell-cum-Starbotton, and a dozen others, or in great, meandering, home counties churchyards glowing with bluebells and wood anemones, such as that of St Peter and Paul at Great Missenden in Buckinghamshire.

In certain churchyards, an exceptional quality of care is immediately obvious. Those who think that a churchyard rich in wildlife must be a scruffy place should visit Littleham in Devon where, down a wooded lane in the valley of the River Yeo, lies the church of St Swithun's. I visited it on May Day in a sunny spring, and it was an experience I shall not forget. Full of flowers, trees and birds, it recalled the garden of the dream in Chaucer's *The Romance of the Rose*. There were all the plants I had come to expect in a good traditional churchyard: bluebells, red campion, primroses, the churchyard pink primrose, speedwells, stitchwort and lady's smock. In taller patches of vegetation, hemp agrimony was coming up along with columbines, cow parsley and foxgloves. There were ramsons, dog's mercury, woodrush, and the clear blue of bugle flowers. The churchyard itself was everything anyone could desire, sheltered and beautifully situated, with several benches where people could sit and enjoy the scene and the singing birds. On either side of the main path to the south porch and around the new graves, the grass was neatly mown, but the way in which the parishioners had managed the rest of this churchyard was extremely interesting. They had worked out, in their own way, a method recommended by professional naturalists for churchyard conservation. Instead of mowing everything flat every few weeks, they kept close-mown only grassy paths which wound their way within the taller grass of the rest of the churchyard which was cut once or twice annually. In the north-east corner, this slightly longer grass was spectacularly laced with the pink-purple of early purple orchids. I counted no less than sixty spikes in flower around the path and even in some of the graves—a healthy colony with every likelihood of continuing to be so, it seems.

The practical work in this churchyard is done by a few parishioners who have divided up the large area between them, each taking responsibility for her or his part. One of their number is a woman who is also something of a botanist, and a painter. Her sketch-book, containing paintings of all the plants she has seen in the churchyard, is kept in the

Deadly nightshade growing from the base of a chest tomb in St Cross churchyard, Holywell, Oxford. All parts of the plant contain extremely poisonous alkaloids, and one name for the shiny black fruits is 'devil's cherries'.

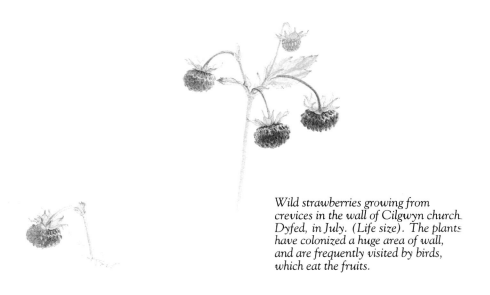

Wild strawberries growing from crevices in the wall of Cilgwyn church, Dyfed, in July. (Life size). The plants have colonized a huge area of wall, and are frequently visited by birds, which eat the fruits.

church in a hewn-out chest, dating from the tenth century, recently found and restored. This book shows the visitor all the plants which appear throughout the year. I would not otherwise have guessed the presence of centaury and betony, two summer-flowering plants not likely to catch the eye earlier in the year.

Another churchyard which demonstrated in every aspect clear concern for its wildlife was St Michael and All Angels at Bugbrooke in Northamptonshire. Hung on one of the great trees near the main path is a small plaque on which is written a quatrain from 'God's Acre' by Longfellow:

I like that ancient Saxon phrase which calls
The burial ground God's Acre! It is just;
It consecrates each grave within its walls
And breathes a benison o'er the sleeping dust.

There are fine, mature lime trees, rooks in the tall beeches, cuckoos calling, lesser celandines and a large patch of lungwort, violets, bluebells, and even one or two delightful, orchid-like double lady's smocks. Near a shrub-lined boundary, I found primroses and wood anemones. A little river skirts the other side. I was told that a small area is to be set aside as a nature reserve

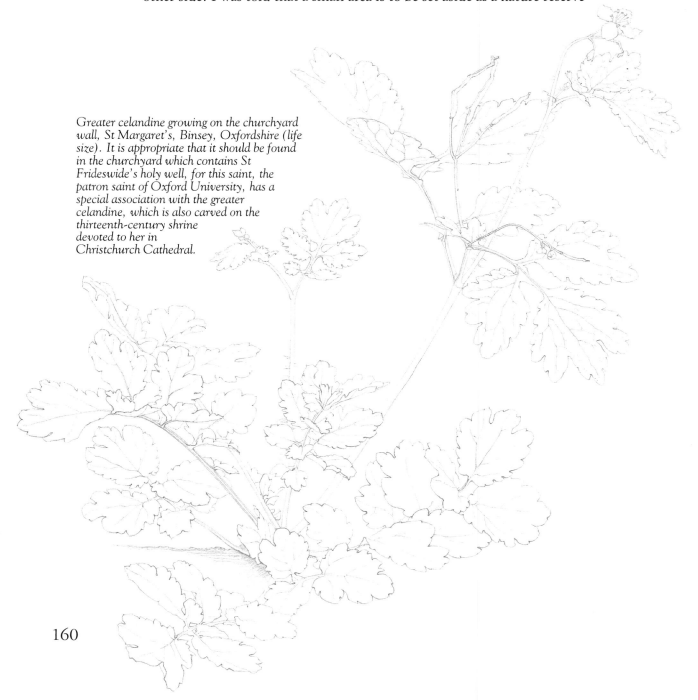

Greater celandine growing on the churchyard wall, St Margaret's, Binsey, Oxfordshire (life size). It is appropriate that it should be found in the churchyard which contains St Frideswide's holy well, for this saint, the patron saint of Oxford University, has a special association with the greater celandine, which is also carved on the thirteenth-century shrine devoted to her in Christchurch Cathedral.

when the churchyard is extended, but in fact, the churchyard as a whole is an excellent nature reserve, though a small wild tangle of taller grass would be welcome. In the belfry one reads the melancholy old couplet, 'I to the church the living call, and to the grave do summon all', a prospect mollified by the nature of this churchyard, and made to seem a not altogether undesirable proposition.

I had been alerted by the Women's Institute churchyard survey to expect something out of the ordinary at both Littleham and Bugbrooke, but my expectations for the churchyard at Bibury in Gloucestershire were extremely depressed. I had been very much put off by Alec Clifton-Taylor's description: 'perhaps the most enchanting churchyard in England . . . There is a wide expanse of faultlessly mown lawn and a few standard roses which look exactly right . . . the efforts of a good gardener have doubled our pleasure.' It sounded like a wildlife desert.

However, when I went there, I found it not as artificial as I had feared. There are mop-topped rose trees, but the putti on the beautiful limestone tombs smile down over orange-gold lichens. The lawns are very extensive, but growing on the walls of church and churchyard are many vivid patches of hartstongue fern, and in their immediate shelter, bushy green alkanet, deep blue germander speedwell and towering pillars of dark mullein. Nearby, under the trees grow feverfew and herb Bennet, the blessed plant (also known as wood avens), woody nightshade and lady's mantle, foxgloves, herb Robert and burdock—all in a not very large and rather too well-kept churchyard. Even the Alice-in-Wonderland roses were not quite as they seemed. Some of the regimented line had died and the ones planted to take their places had been muddled, so that the red-white alternation had gone awry. (However, there were no distraught footmen attempting to paint the white roses red.)

Greater celandine leaves are a soft grey-green.

A shrivelled seed pod.

Flowers are like tiny poppies.

161

The man who does the gardening in this churchyard and has done so for eight years, told me he had never given much thought to the churchyard as a place of wildlife—but that, nevertheless, he disliked weed-killers and simply cut the grass around graves. He volunteered, too, that he always mowed around wild flowers. It pleased him to hear the song of the birds and he had seen kingfishers flying over the churchyard. An ardent botanist, birdwatcher or entomologist would no doubt be dissatisfied, but in the context of the Cotswolds, where every house and tidy garden is a picturesque showpiece, this churchyard was managed, I thought, in a remarkably humane way.

When people say that they mow around wild flowers, they usually mean the well-loved flowers of meadow, wayside and woodland such as cowslips, primroses, foxgloves, ramsons or bluebells. People take a natural delight in these plants; one finds small islands of bloom in even the tidiest of town churchyards. Though cutting back after flowering may be hasty, not allowing the plants time to make seed, it is extremely unusual for anyone to mow such flowers in bloom. In only one of all my churchyard explorations have I seen it, and I feel sure that the soggy disagreeable mess of grass and mashed daffodil must have given rise to enough adverse comment in the parish for it not to occur again. However, protection does not usually extend to inconspicuous, less well-known wild flowers. An unusual hawkweed, for instance, which might be of considerable botanical interest, would very likely be seen simply as a dandelion-like weed.

A difficulty which faces churchyard conservation at present is that often neither the incumbent nor anyone in the parochial church council is aware of what they have in their churchyard, nor what methods of management are open to them. Even when botanists have made a full survey of the churchyard, the local people may be entirely unaware, not only of the results, but that it has been done at all. When they are given such information, the response is characteristically one of interest and concern. In a churchyard in Morden, Surrey, gravestone clearance was halted and some of the best stones were saved after a lichenologist contacted the vicar and pointed out how rich in species some of the memorials were. Members of one Durham church changed their attitude towards bats on learning something about them from a local Bat Group representative and finding they were giving harbour to a whiskered bat, rare so far north.

Honeysuckle berries in a Suffolk churchyard at the end of July. (Life size).

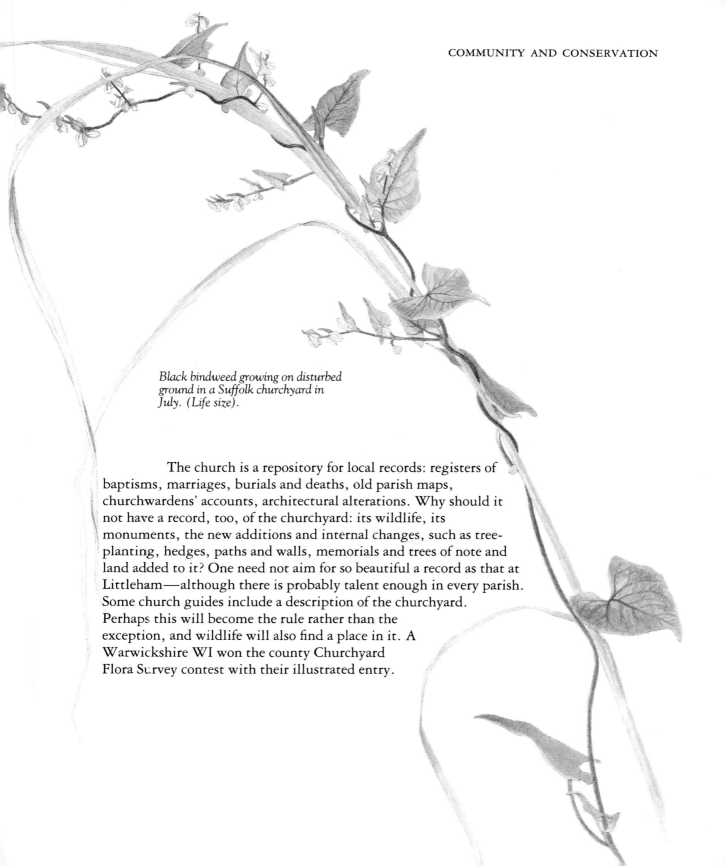

*Black bindweed growing on disturbed
ground in a Suffolk churchyard in
July. (Life size).*

The church is a repository for local records: registers of
baptisms, marriages, burials and deaths, old parish maps,
churchwardens' accounts, architectural alterations. Why should it
not have a record, too, of the churchyard: its wildlife, its
monuments, the new additions and internal changes, such as tree-
planting, hedges, paths and walls, memorials and trees of note and
land added to it? One need not aim for so beautiful a record as that at
Littleham—although there is probably talent enough in every parish.
Some church guides include a description of the churchyard.
Perhaps this will become the rule rather than the
exception, and wildlife will also find a place in it. A
Warwickshire WI won the county Churchyard
Flora Survey contest with their illustrated entry.

Identifying the particular composition of wildlife in any one churchyard helps in its way to ensure that it is cared for and that the individual nature of that churchyard is preserved. Each has its own particular character and it would be so much better to have maintenance which is sensitive to this, and to the needs and resources of the parish, than the present trend towards bland, close-shaved mediocrity and uniformity.

While the parishioners quite reasonably expect a trim, well-kept churchyard, there are only a very few, if any, who are actually able to help with the practical maintenance. It is not surprising that the parochial church councils—who are locally responsible for churchyard upkeep—are influenced by horticultural marketing, which plays heavily on labour-saving claims, and they turn gratefully to rotary mowers, strimmers and chemical weed-killers in an effort to fulfil their task. They, and those who actually carry out the work, sincerely believe that in making the churchyard garden-like they are doing their best for it. It is readily assumed, as a parish magazine from mid-Wales put it, that a 'churchyard which has flowerbeds and a closely clipped lawn with tidy gravestones' is an indication of a healthy and vital parish life. In this context, it is not cleanliness that is regarded as next to godliness, but tidiness. Anything which seems remotely scruffy is removed; gravestones are scraped bare of their lichens and weed-killers assiduously applied around their bases, ivy is ripped from walls, and every week during the growing season, the whine of grass-cutting machinery fills the air. The result of all this activity resembles the aristocratic churchyard described by Thomas Hardy in *A Pair of Blue Eyes*:

> Here the grass was carefully tended, and formed virtually a part of the manor-house lawn; flowers and shrubs being planted indiscriminately over both, whilst the few graves visible were mathematically exact in shape and smoothness, appearing in the day-time like chins newly shaven. There was no wall, the division between God's Acre and Lord Luxellian's being marked only by a few square stones . . .

Ironically, churchyards maintained to these standards are still labour-intensive when compared with more traditional ones. However, in the nineteenth century only someone of Lord Luxellian's wealth could afford the

Common toad under tree roots in the redundant churchyard, Corpusty, Norfolk, in May.

exercise, whereas the existence of modern horticultural equipment has
brought it within the aspirations of any parish which is able to raise the
capital outlay. The question is, of course, whether such highly gardened
churchyards are desirable. The idea that the churchyard is a reflection on the
community can perhaps be used as an argument against this kind of
churchyard and in support of conservation. The seminar organized by The
Prince of Wales' Committee in 1982 on the subject of churchyards and
chapelyards in Wales concluded that projects which resulted in the
destruction of wildlife habitats and the removal or breaking up of
gravestones created a churchyard which was 'as much an adverse comment
as one overgrown with scrub'.

For the parish itself, the benefits of a shaved and shorn churchyard
are dubious—in terms of the practicalities, let alone the aesthetics. Those
who diligently try to keep an acre or more as fastidiously tidy as their own
gardens create an enormous amount of work for themselves, and for their
successors, if such can be found. Gardens demand continuous care and

if this is interrupted by reason of illness, death or people moving away, the lawn will not regain its former wild flowers, but will become overgrown with invasive and unsightly species such as nettles, dock and ground elder. I met a churchwarden almost in despair over a churchyard frontage which had grown rank in less than three months, while the churchyard mower had been away for repairs. The rear of the churchyard which was given less frequent attention was pleasant with the sound of bees and grasshoppers. Several different grasses were in flower and in among them the yellows of meadow vetchling, bird's-foot trefoil, and buttercups gleamed brightly; hogweed, the tallest of all the coarse-meadow flowers, grew in sturdy clumps, its off-white saucers soaking in the afternoon sun.

In many of the WI surveys there was a sense of ambivalence towards manicured churchyards, caught in the phrase of an East Sussex member who wrote that her parish churchyard was too well-kept for wild flowers to grow. There was certainly an awareness of the relationship between the kind of management practised and wildlife. A survey from Devon noted bleakly that since the acquisition of a new strimmer and brush-cutter, there had been no voles, frogs, or toads, grass snakes or lizards seen in the churchyard. Slow-worms are another creature very vulnerable to the speed and violence of strimmers and rotary mowers. An additional disadvantage of these machines is that they do not collect the mowings; left to rot, these look untidy and return to the soil nutrients which begin to change the meadow balance of the land in the same way that applying fertilizer does, encouraging a few species at the expense of diversity.

However, the impression given by the surveys was by no means entirely dismal. In some places, an awareness of wildlife had led to practical conservation measures being taken. Several churchyards deliberately set

Bumble bee on birdsfoot trefoil (above), and small pearl-bordered fritillary (right).

aside an area of long grass to provide a habitat for butterflies and grasshoppers. Many surveys mentioned the butterflies which frequent the churchyard: the yellow brimstone, the subtler tones of the meadow, wall and hedge browns, the colourful small tortoiseshell and peacock, the dramatic comma and the dainty blues. It seemed, however, that although they were very much welcomed, the butterflies' needs in terms of food plants and egg-laying sites were hardly appreciated at all. There were exceptions, such as West Runton churchyard in Norfolk, where sorrel plants are retained as food

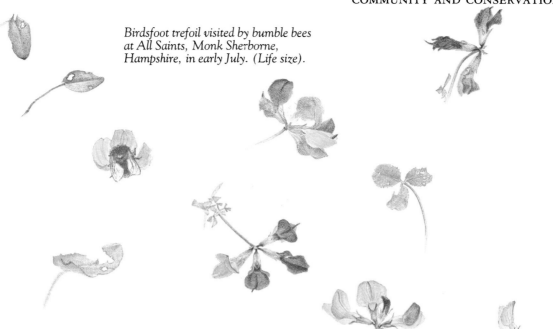

Birdsfoot trefoil visited by bumble bees at All Saints, Monk Sherborne, Hampshire, in early July. (Life size).

for the small copper butterfly. As the churchyard survey of butterflies, underway in Norfolk and Lincolnshire, progresses, the situation should improve.

Birds are given special consideration in some churchyards. In Bugbrooke and many other places, there are nestboxes on the trees. Several surveys mentioned the pride in having a resident owl, especially if it was a barn owl. This is the only bird whose presence is tolerated inside the church; the vicar of St Trinity's, Crockham Hill in Kent claimed he could hear their owl snoring through his sermons. Swifts, swallows and house martins are usually welcome on the outer fabric of the church, and at Caister-on-Sea in Norfolk, where the swallows nest in the porch, the church cleaners solved the problem of their droppings with an improvised dirt tray of newspaper weighted down with sand, which is regularly replaced.

Bats are less popular than birds, though interest in them is increasing. Those who are responsible for cleaning the church tend to dislike roosting colonies because both brass and wood are stained by their urine. Placing drapes in vulnerable spots keeps the problem at bay, but I wish every success to the church helper who is experimenting in the hope of finding a protective polish which will solve the problem.

The greatest threat to the traditional churchyard is not a new one. Thomas Hardy wrote 'The Levelled Churchyard' in 1882:

O Passenger, pray list and catch
    Our sighs and piteous groans,
Half stifled in this jumbled patch
    Of wrenched memorial stones!

We late-lamented, resting here,
    Are mixed to human jam,
And each to each exclaims in fear,
    "I know not which I am!"

The wicked people have annexed
    The verses on the good;
A roaring drunkard sports the text
    Teetotal Tommy should!

Where we are huddled none can trace,
    And if our names remain,
They pave some path or porch or place
    Where we have never lain!

Here's not a modest maiden elf
    But dreads the final Trumpet,
Lest half of her should rise herself,
    And half some sturdy strumpet!

From restorations of Thy fane,
    From smoothings of Thy sward,
From zealous Churchmen's pick and plane
    Deliver us O Lord! Amen!

[fane = temple]

The business of totally clearing the churchyard—of gravestones, kerbs, even the grave mounds, has accelerated with the increased investment in modern mowing machinery. One thing these mowing machines cannot do is to cut close to graves with headstones or kerbs. Some mowers of churchyards simply steer around the graves, leaving tufts of long grass, ferns and wild flowers to be dealt with, or not, as those who tend the graves see fit. From a practical point of view (and a naturalist's) this seems a comfortable compromise, but in many churchyards an even flat turf is desired throughout, and nothing less will do. When the headstones go, so does the shelter they provide. When the ground is flattened, the small micro-habitat of the grave mound becomes a uniform part of the lawn.

The headstones themselves are generally dragged away to be stacked in a pile, or leant against the church wall. Sometimes they are used for paving, which quickly wears away the inscriptions, making investigation very difficult for local historians. Headstones are an important aid to the historian in the traditional churchyard, especially in Wales, where parish records were not generally kept until 1812. One of the few ways the historian can guess at the social relationships and the status of families and individuals in past centuries is to examine the juxtapositions of the grave memorials in the church and chapel yards. Some parishes re-site their headstones in neat lines elsewhere in the churchyard, but this is only slightly preferable to the other alternatives, since the original relationships between graves are lost—as may be the lichen growth of centuries.

A conservation conflict—ivy can shade lichens out of existence and hide epitaphs, but it provides a recess for snails and other creatures. These gravestones are in St Clement's churchyard, Oxford.

169

In any consideration of the management of what may be a very large acreage of grass in a churchyard, it would obviously be absurd to preach against any and all use of motor mowers. While the symbolic figure of Death with his long scythe may habitually walk the poetic churchyard, helpful volunteers who have the skill of this implement and are prepared to put it to use in cutting the churchyard sward are few and far between. Motor mowers are easy to use and when brought into action at sensible intervals help to keep churchyards both trim, and healthy for wildlife.

The scythe is used when the grass is high in late June or July, and the cut can be gathered in for hay. I was notified of only one churchyard, at All Saints, Smallbridge, Devon, where a scythe was still regularly used to cut a part of it, but in several others the churchyard grass was cut for hay. I visited Dulas in Herefordshire, where the churchyard of St Michael contains a rich combination of ancient meadow plants—delicious hay for some lucky beasts. At Grundisburgh in Suffolk, an additional piece of land acquired for the churchyard as burial ground (but not yet used) was also cut for hay. At Morton-cum-Grafton in North Yorkshire, hay-making took place within living memory, and at Wingrave in Buckinghamshire, hay from the churchyard used to be used in the rush-strewing ceremony. Haymaking seems to be well into decline in the present day, but perhaps with renewed interest in old forms of management a change in direction may occur. Certainly, there are few more satisfying sights than watching the tall grasses in an ancient meadow fall silently to the rhythmic beat of the scythe.

Meadow cranesbill at Asthall churchyard, Oxfordshire, in late July (life size). The fruits explode, dispersing the seeds well away from the parent plant.

The other well-established method of dealing with grass and awkward undergrowth in a churchyard is to graze it, and this is a method which seems to be gaining popularity. In my travels, I have seen goats and small groups of sheep, and heard of other grazing animals: donkeys in Yorkshire, a heifer belonging to the vicar of a Norfolk church, ponies in the New Forest, even mallards, and churchyard geese. There is also a host of unauthorized grazers, principally rabbits, but also hares and deer.

Churchyard grazing is an ancient practice. For centuries, there have been factions to support it while others fought against it. Traditionally, parishioners have the right to burial in the churchyard, but the incumbent has the grazing rights or herbage. He could also, if he so wished, let out his grazing rights to others and now, as in the past, this seems acceptable unless the right is seriously abused. Archdeacon Hale's *Precedents and Proceedings illustrative of the Discipline of the Church of England* cites two extreme examples which came before the ecclesiastical courts of the sixteenth century. The first was a complaint from the parishioners of a certain Ardeby, who accused the parson and the vicar of letting the churchyard 'to them that usethe it wythe vile bestes', (probably pigs, which are unwelcome because they rootle as well as graze). A case was brought a few years later, against the rector of Langdon Hull, who was summoned to explain to the court why he had allowed sheep to be folded inside the church. He successfully defended himself by proving that this had been the only means of saving the animals when a heavy and unexpected fall of snow had endangered their lives, and that they had in any case been there for only 'two workinge dayes'. There are mildly approving recommendations for judicious grazing in several church handbooks dating from the nineteenth century to the present day.

Billy goats resting and browsing holly in St Martin's churchyard, Litchborough, Northamptonshire; by ancient tradition, the rector has the right to keep four goats or six sheep in this churchyard.

In order to protect graves from being trampled and soiled by grazing animals, it is thought that parishioners once pegged out new graves with brambles or willows. George Crabbe describes 'humble graves, with wickers bound' in his poem 'Sir Eustace Grey' and the practice receives fuller elaboration in the quatrain from John Gay's 'Dirge':

> With wicker rods we fenc'd her Tomb around,
> To ward from Man and Beast the hallow's ground:
> Lest her new Grave the Parson's Cattle raze,
> For both his Horse and Cow the church Yard graze.

There is a clause in the will of a parishioner at Braughing in Hertfordshire, in 1696, which enjoined that his grave be annually 'brambled'. Another famous example is the pre-Raphaelite painting by Arthur Hughes, *Home from the Sea*, which shows sheep in the churchyard, and the young boy's prostrate form echoed in the shape of a simple construction of withies over the grave behind him. It has always struck me that the frail constructions in this picture would be no match for a sheep; Thomas Hardy's 'tight mounds bounded by sticks, which shout imprisonment' has a truer ring. The wealthy would purchase from a huge choice of cast iron surrounds, custom-made for the grave plot, which made a more effective barrier.

Sheep may safely graze nowadays in many churchyards, even the famous Ingworth and Blickling pedigree flock of black mountain sheep, prized for their fine dense wool, and whose fame reaches far beyond their Norfolk home. Grazing is widespread but, I believe, accepted as the principal means of grass control only in parts of Wales. It seems to have been more common in the past, when churchyard sheep were sometimes

Sheep grazing in the shade of a yew tree in a fenced-off area of St Mary's churchyard, Speen, Berkshire, on a bright August day.

owned by the incumbent or jointly by the parish. At Hannington in Hampshire, sheep were penned in the churchyard before they were sheared, and in the porch of Holy Trinity church at Balsham in Cambridgeshire, there are holes for hurdles which excluded sheep from the church. Nowadays, sheep are allowed to range unconfined in some churchyards, though this mainly occurs where there are no recent graves. In churchyards where burials still take place, the modern methods of limiting the animals are to erect a large-mesh wire fence pinned to posts or electric fencing.

Even a traditional method of grass control, such as sheep-grazing, should be permitted with a certain amount of caution. Sheep have been called 'mowers on four legs' and the comparison is apt. The overgrazing which occurs when there are too many sheep for the area, or when they are grazed continuously, is as damaging as excessive mowing. Dividing a large churchyard into plots and moving the sheep around from one to another through the spring and summer may be an answer. Another solution is to let them graze only at controlled intervals, giving the plants a chance to flower and seed themselves.

It is unfortunate that, while it is reasonably simple to keep a traditional churchyard in good order, once the original ground flora has been reduced, it takes a degree of commitment and hard work to restore it to a reasonably healthy condition. Some of the plants will not be seen there again, unless they are brought in and planted. Some botanists strongly object to replenishing the churchyard with plants, but where there is a sensible plan and adequate care with the choice of species and the planting, it can achieve remarkable results.

A major difficulty in advancing the idea of churchyard conservation has been the struggle against an element of popular opinion. For the 'Best Kept Churchyard' competitions of the nineteen-seventies and early nineteen-eighties, interpret simply 'tidiest churchyard'. Even in 1984 the village of Scothern in Lincolnshire which, having entered for the 'Best Kept Village' competition, was marked down by the judges for 'an untidy corner in their churchyard'. The corner in question was an area which had deliberately been left untouched as a conservation area to encourage butterflies and birds. However, following contact made by the local officer of the British Butterfly Conservation Society with The Council for the Preservation of Rural England, there may be recommendations about conservation initiatives. Although the Best Kept Village competition is held under the auspices of the Council for the Protection of Rural England, each county has its own separate organization and the criteria are not standardized. In some counties conservation is already a consideration. The village of Staplefield, which has twice won the Sussex title, was awarded points for the care it took of its churchyard orchids.

On a national level the care of churchyards has been a matter of concern to the Church in Wales, which is the only body at present seeking to exercise control over the graveyards for which it has responsibility (this leaves aside those managed by chapels and local authorites). The 1982 seminar of the Prince of Wales' Committee (a registered charity concerned

Carved stone butterfly and snail (above and below) on a tomb in St Brynach's churchyard, Nevern, Dyfed, together with a real common garden snail (right).

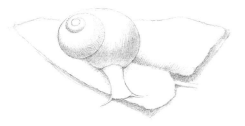

with the Welsh environment) was held specifically 'to discuss the increasing number of ill-advised projects taking place in burial places, particularly in churchyards and chapelyards throughout Wales'. Regarding the removal of gravestones it recognizes that 'churchyards are important for archaeological, aesthetic and ecological reasons, and their character should be retained for future generations'. The main findings and conclusions of the seminar are summarized well in a five-page leaflet published in 1984 and which gives ideas and guidelines for the upkeep of graveyards.

By far the most enterprising practical churchyard scheme is that initiated by the Northamptonshire Naturalists' Trust in collaboration with the county's Rural Community Council. They offer advice to any parochial church council in their region on how to manage a churchyard with respect for wildlife. They also run a churchyard competition and measure the entrants, not in terms of tidiness (though neatness is a consideration), but in terms of conservation and richness of wildlife. The judges' comments also include suggestions for improvement. When I visited the first winners of this competition (begun in 1983) at Woodford on the hillside above the River Nene, it was clear that many of the suggestions had been taken to heart. As suggested, the grass mowings had been raked up, grass paths through the churchyard were close-mown and clearly defined, and the policy of maintaining medium length and, in unobtrusive corners, long grass had been continued. It is a most attractive churchyard, neat, but full of tremendously healthy and varied wild flowers, grave plantings, introduced and native trees. Birdsong seemed to come from almost every tree and the warm, delicious, resiny scent of the balsam poplar planted by the entrance lingered in the air.

Litchborough churchyard, which earned the Northamptonshire prize in the year this book was written, was exceptional, even to its walls. On them grows common polypody, herb Robert, germander speedwell, ivy-leaved toadflax and several other plants, the most interesting of which is navelwort, a rare occurrence so far east. A devil which is half goat is a common characterization of Old Nick, but nothing could have been further from this than the serene and handsome white goats tethered firmly to gravestones in this churchyard. They peer gently around to observe anyone entering the churchyard and then return to the business of consuming all the vegetation within reach. A map in the church porch shows how the churchyard has been divided into eight sections which are managed on a rotational basis. The area grazed by goats this year will be allowed in the next to grow to high grass for hay. The grass on either side of the path to the church is always kept close-mown and a far corner is left mostly untouched for the benefit of butterflies and grasshoppers. There are high hedges and plenty of well-grown trees and shrubs. The plants in this churchyard are a particular pleasure to the eye, in form as well as colour. Not having been continually chopped back, they have developed their own shapes. There are roses which really ramble, towering foxgloves and a good bushy patch of comfrey. An ex-grave plant, the willow-leaved bellflower, with flowers of deepest blue, was managing to flower bravely in the turf. On and around the church walls alone, there are twenty species of flowering plants and ferns: plants as varied as mullein and the small, dense cushions of pearlwort, made up of bright green thread-like stems and tiny leaves (which offered a chance for keen botanists to compare two species—annual and procumbent pearlwort). The ivy makes patterns along the wall behind spiny-leaved teasel and the delicate foliage of columbine, and chickweed sprawls bright green on the ground.

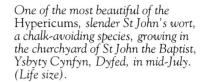

One of the most beautiful of the Hypericums, slender St John's wort, a chalk-avoiding species, growing in the churchyard of St John the Baptist, Ysbyty Cynfyn, Dyfed, in mid-July. (Life size).

There are plants of the woodland, meadow, hedgerow, lawn and of rock and garden habitats, all looked after with evident care and understanding. Non-flowering plants such as liverworts, mosses and lichens also made a good showing, and a dead stump, covered in ivy, had been left to provide a habitat for saphrophytes.

The moving spirit behind this remarkable churchyard is a rare individual who combines a sense of what is appropriate for a churchyard with a strong appreciation of natural history. The result is almost ideal: a churchyard in the centre of the village which is as attractive to people as it is to wildlife. When I arrived at Litchborough in the hard glare of the summer's afternoon, the lightly shaded entrance to the churchyard beckoned an invitation I could never have resisted. In *Nature in Downland* over eighty years ago, W.H. Hudson wrote of how 'often during a long walk over the downs in hot weather' he thought of the church and churchyard 'as of a shaded fountain in a parched desert'. So they still seem to many of us.

Common toadflax (life size), a familiar of churchyards and hedgerows, at Cley next the Sea, Norfolk, in late August.

APPENDIX I

EVERY CHURCHYARD HAS ITS OWN individual character and interest—it usually takes several visits to appreciate fully what each holds. These two surveys, from mid-Wales and Derbyshire, illustrate the kind of picture which emerges from close observation and research in the churchyards concerned.

EGLWYS NEWYDD (HAFOD) CHURCHYARD, DYFED
Arthur Chater

Arthur Chater works in the Botany Department of the British Museum (Natural History). He is also Recorder for the botanical vice-county of Cardiganshire and has for many years had a keen interest in churchyards and their conservation. He has published both on the natural history of churchyards and on the subject of gravestones.

EGLWYS NEWYDD IS NOT BY ANY means the richest in species of the hundred churchyards in the Ceredigion district of Dyfed, or the most varied in habitat—nor are the rarest plants contained within it, but it perfectly represents the balance between nature and human activity that makes a good churchyard such a delight. It is still as George Eyre Evans, a local historian, described it in 1903 'a veritable "God's Acre",—calm, restful, picturesque, and well-kept'.

The second highest churchyard in Ceredigion, it is situated on a steep south-east facing slope in the Ystwyth valley. The first church on the site was built in 1620 to serve both the local lead mining community and the Herbert family at the mansion of Hafod Ychtryd in the valley. Thomas Johnes, a later owner of Hafod, had the church rebuilt in 1803. The Forestry Commission now owns much of the Hafod estate and their conifer plantations now enclose the churchyard on three sides.

Many of the plants and animals found in this churchyard are tokens of its earlier history. Two large pedunculate oaks flanking the path to the church, together with three others beyond the church, must have been among the five million trees, half of them oaks, that Thomas Johnnes planted on his estate about 1800. Few are now left standing. One oak has been so severely lopped that it is little more than a bristly trunk—but a haven for birds and innumerable insects. Winter moths swarm on its trunk and twigs on frosty December nights. Around the church are six yews, the three largest measuring about 410cm in girth. Yews of this size are usually well over 300 years old and one can assume these were planted when the church was founded. Two of them are fused together at the base, giving the appearance of a great forked trunk.

The grassland is varied and surprisingly undisturbed, although there are graves all over the churchyard. Above the entrance path it is heathy, with ling, blaeberry and heath bedstraw among the fescue and sweet vernal grass—and there are no fewer than five different ferns. The clumps of lady and male fern which unfurl their new fronds so quickly after having been cut, are one of the chief delights. The slope below the path is damper and the vegetation consists of tall herbs such as meadow sweet, sorrel and pignut, a relic of the unimproved meadows that are now so hard to find in this neighbourhood. Shaded by yews and the crowded conifers which surround the churchyard, the level damp turf to the south-west of the chancel contains the plants of a damp woodland clearing: lady's smock, wood sorrel, marsh thistle and yellow pimpernel. (Is this a relic of a plant community dating from before the development of the churchyard?) Further south-west there is rich heath flora, harebell, wavy hair-grass, tuberous bitter vetch, heath bedstraw and wood sage—similar to that on the few remaining rocky ungrazed slopes elsewhere in this valley.

Many of the graves are covered with sandy gravel from the nearby lead mines, so toxic that only certain kinds of plant can survive. A resistant form of bent grass grows on some and one of them used to have a resistant form of sea campion which developed on the polluted spoil heaps of the mines from plants which spread up the rivers from the coast to these beach-like habitats, and was brought into the churchyard with the gravel. Other graves have on them comparatively unpolluted river gravel, and these are carpeted with the upright whitish lichen *Cladonia furcata*. Hedge bedstraw grows in the turf of one grave—a lime-loving plant, inexplicably frequent in the predominantly acid churchyards in Ceredigion, and very rare outside them. The naturalized flora includes Welsh poppy, snowdrops, creeping jenny, fox-and-cubs and wild daffodils.

The old dry stone walls are densely covered with mosses and lichens. Tussocks of wood meadow grass, smooth meadow grass and polypody fern grow from the vertically set coping stones. On the walls and elsewhere in the churchyard is a conspicuous yellow hawkweed *Hieracium grandidens*, a rare introduced species known only in Ceredigion from this churchyard and nearby walls.

Most of the headstones are made from local grit-stone or shale or North Wales slate, and there are others of Forest of Dean stone and sandstone. All are well populated with lichens, except for memorials of granite whose polished surfaces are devoid of any life. Marble can look out of keeping amongst vernacular stone, but being limestone, it can have biological compensations. One particular marble headstone is pleasantly disguised by a film of greenish algae which I observed one night being grazed by a total of 19 brown-lipped snails *Cepaea nemoralis* (which in this churchyard are pure yellow, lacking the usual brown or black bands), two tree slugs *Limax marginatus* and no fewer than 84 specimens of a species of woodlouse *Philoscia muscorum*. Two of another species *Oniscus asellus* were feeding on the bird droppings on top of the stone, and at its base were 24 individuals of the tiny chrysalis snail *Lauria cylindracea* which are abundant in this churchyard. The common garden snail *Helix aspersa* is also present. The best way to observe such creatures is to go out on a damp, mild night with a torch and to shine it on the headstones.

The larger animals of the churchyard are more difficult to spot, but at night, I have seen a polecat crossing a path, a palmate newt on the rim of a yellow brick grave enclosure, a frog, a hedgehog and voles. The birds treat this graveyard as if it were a clearing in the forest. There are goldcrests in the yews, nuthatches on the oaks and buzzards and ravens overhead.

A high-walled memorial enclosure to Thomas Johnes and his family is filled to overflowing by a great rhododendron which in early June is an incandescent mass of crimson flowers. Across the path is the grave of the last squire of Hafod, T. J. Waddingham (died 1938), who left to the church the acre of land to the north-east, which was officially incorporated into the churchyard in 1978. Laboriously cleared of its oak woodland and subsequent growth of scrub, this part was sprayed with *asulam* to clear the bracken. This killed the bracken and appeared to do little harm to the rest of the vegetation, and revealed a vast population of bluebells, a relic from the old woodland, and a glorious sight in late May (everything is later than usual at this altitude). Scrub has again formed on the slope above the bluebells: hazel, birch, a thicket of brambles and wild raspberries, sycamore saplings and even a sweet chestnut. Bracken is re-invading from both above and below but is not yet a serious problem.

Eglwys Newydd churchyard has benefitted from a job creation scheme. Paths were improved, leaning gravestones straightened and the place brought up to scratch without harm to its natural vegetation, but such schemes usually happen only once, and the regular maintenance often stretches the resources of the parish to the utmost. In some years the grass has been cut once only, but in 1983 five sheep were given the run of the churchyard with very satisfactory results. Constant grazing, though, would of course make the churchyard as dull and poor in species as the nearby sheepwalks above the forest. As it is there are about 120 species of flowering plants and ferns in this churchyard, and thanks to the way it has been tended it is one of the most beautiful and interesting sites in the valley.

ST OSWALD'S PARISH CHURCH, ASHBOURNE, DERBYSHIRE
K. M. Hollick

Miss Kathleen Hollick has lived for many years in an old house next to the churchyard in the market town of Ashbourne in Derbyshire. Her late father established plants in it, and she has given advice on its management, especially with regard to grass-cutting. At present, West Derbyshire Council is responsible for the maintenance, and carries it out very satisfactorily—waiting until plants such as daffodils die back before cutting, for instance. Miss Hollick is Recorder for the botanical vice-county of Derbyshire.

THE AVENUE OF LIMES was planted early 19th century and pleached. Mostly common lime, a few small-leaved and there were some large-leaved. The row on the north side of the vicar's walk is being felled by the local council—being roadside and about at the end of their lives.

The church has a 'weeping' chancel, that is crooked. The daffodils were planted by the late Dr H.H. Hollick over the period 1910–40. He also in the 1930s planted the bluebells—including many Spanish bluebell (*Endymion hispanicus*) in blue, pink and white (and hybrids with common bluebell *Endymion non-scriptus* are present in plenty). The snowdrops he planted also at this time, have all done well. The most numerous daffodil is the cultivar 'Emperor'; and 'Cervantes'. 'Victoria' and an old bi-colour are also present. ('White Lady', 'Lucifer', 'Conspicuous' and 'Tresserve' are also present.) *Narcissus poeticus ornatus*, a cultivar of poet's narcissus and *ornatus recurvus* ('Old Pheasant's eye') grow to the north of the church, a few *N. asturiensis* (a very small species) occur east of the chancel by the path, and there are wild daffodils (*N. pseudo-narcissus*) in the south section.

Some blue anemones (*Anemone appenina*) were planted by the late Mr Peveril Turnbull early this century, and did well for many years, though they are declining now. Dr Hollick planted dog daisies in the 1940s and these have thrived and multiplied to make a splendid sight, especially in the east section where bulbous buttercup and meadow clover are also excellent. There is often an odd clump of harebells growing in the church walls on the south side and they are also to be found in the close-mown grass south of the chancel.

Some years ago there was a good colony of quaking grass north-west of Spalden's almhouses—gone now unfortunately. When the great Cambridge botanist John Ray visited Ashbourne in 1670, he recorded hairy rock-cress (*Arabis hirsuta*) on the church walls—none observed in living memory.

Other good meadow flowers include hogweed, pignut, goat's beard, greater burnet saxifrage. There was much sweet violet in the shade of the cedar of Lebanon before it lost nearly all of its branches in the heavy snows of 1940—now all gone—though the remains of the cedar are still there: planted c. 1840. Some nice wood anemone to the north of the nave. Mosses present include *Thuidium tamariscinum*, *Tortula muralis* and *Brachythecium rutabulum*.

APPENDIX II

A SELECTION OF PLANTS WITH RELIGIOUS NAMES AND ASSOCIATIONS.

Abraham, Isaac and Jacob	Comfrey and lungwort are both given this name because they have flowers of different colours (ranging from pink to blue) on the same plant.
Adam and Eve	Lungwort (as above Abraham, Isaac and Jacob) and also early purple orchid, spotted orchid, lords and ladies (possibly because of double tubers but more likely because of different flower colours either on the same plant or within a colony).
Angel's eyes	Germander speedwell, because the flowers are as blue as the sky.
Apostles	Star of Bethlehem.
Archangel	Yellow archangel and, less commonly, red deadnettle.
Bats-in-the-belfry	Nettle-leaved bellflower, possibly because of the way the flowers are clustered on the branches up the stem.
Blessed thistle	Milk thistle, more commonly (Our) Lady's thistle (see below).
Cain and Abel	Early purple orchid and marsh orchids (see Adam and Eve). Pluralized—columbines.
Candlemas bells	Snowdrops because of their time of flowering in February. (Candlemas is 2nd February.)
Candlemas caps	Wood anemone, for the same reason as above.
Christians	Bullace, the wild plum tree, used to describe the fruits.
Christmas tree, Christmas, Christ's thorn	Holly, always regarded as a powerful plant and adopted into Christianity from pagan origins.
Christ's ladder	Common centaury.
Church broom	Teasel, because the shape of the flowerhead resembled the broom used to sweep high places.
Church steeples	Agrimony, because of the form of the flower spike.
Churchwort	Pennyroyal, possibly strewn in churches where its sweet scent and flea repellant properties would be appreciated.
Easter bell, Easter flower	Greater stitchwort, because of the time of flowering.
Easter Ledger, Easter ledges, Easter mangiant, Easter mentgions, Easter hedges	Bistort, used in Easter ledger pudding, apparently still eaten in the Lake District, said to aid conception. It begins to bloom in June, later than Easter, so Geoffrey Grigson (in *The Englishman's Flora*) is probably right in believing Easter ledger to be a corruption of *Aristolochia*, birthwort, which also aided conception and delivery.

183

Easter lily, Easter rose	Daffodil, because of the time of flowering. Primrose is also called Easter rose in Somerset.
Eve's cushion	Mossy saxifrage.
Eve's tears	Snowdrop.
God Almighty's bread and cheese	Wood sorrel, from the edible leaves.
God Almighty's flowers, God Almighty's thumb and finger	Bird's-foot trefoil from the trefoil leaf and the finger-like pod.
God's eye	Germander speedwell (see angel's eyes above).
God's finger and thumbs	Fumitory, perhaps from the elongated shape of the flowers.
God's grace	Field wood-rush.
God's meat	Hawthorn, from the young edible leaves.
God's stinking tree	Elder was supposed to have been used for the cross.
Gratia dei, Grace of God	Meadow cranesbill.
Good Friday flower	Townhall clock (moschatel), from the time of flowering.
Good Friday plant	Lungwort, a plant with many religious associations, in flower at this time.
Herb Bennet	In French *herbe de Saint-Benoît*, also 'the blessed herb' in Somerset. The root has a sweet, spicy scent and this fragrance was supposed to repel evil.
Herb Robert	*Herba Sancti Ruperti* or *Herba Roberti* in mediaeval Latin, a plant dedicated to St Robert (St Robert of Salzburg?) but also associated with the magic of Robin Goodfellow.
Holy grass	*Hierochloë odorata*, a rare aromatic grass.
Holy herb	Vervain, believed to be very powerful against devils and demons of disease.
Holy innocents	Hawthorn.
Holy water sprinkle	Horsetails, from the old holy water brush which resembled these plants.
Keys of heaven	Cowslip—from the resemblance of the flowers to old-fashioned keys.
Ladder to heaven	Solomon's seal (see page 73).
Lady Mary's tears, Virgin Mary's milkdrops	Lungwort, the leaves of which are spotted white, traditionally where the drops of Mary's milk fell on them.
Lady's bedstraw	There are many plants prefixed 'lady's' denoting a plant dedicated to Our Lady. She has been given a whole range of domestic accoutrements represented by plants e.g. comb, cloak, mantle, cushion, glove, hatpins etc. The commonest churchyard plants only are mentioned here, among which ranks lady's bedstraw, a very familiar plant of churchyards almost everywhere in England and Wales.

Lady's cowslip	Yellow star of Bethlehem.
Lady's mantle	Native and garden *Alchemilla*.
Lady's smock	The Christian aspect of a plant whose other associations are with cuckoos and springtime loving and promiscuity. Our Lady's smock (the garment) was one of the relics which St Helena found in the cave at Bethlehem.
Lady's thistle	Milk thistle, from the white veins on the leaves caused when the Virgin's milk splashed on to them.
Lady's tresses	So called because the stem with flowers winding up the autumn lady's tresses resembles a braid of hair.
Lent lily, Lent cups, Lents, Lent pitchers, Lenty lily	Wild daffodil, because of the time of flowering.
Marybuds	Mary names are associated with the Virgin Mary. Marybuds is used for several species of buttercup and for marsh marigolds, also called Marybout, and Mary's gold.
Mourning widow	Dusky cranesbill.
Parson-in-his smock, Parson-in-the-pulpit, Parson pillycods, Priest-in-the-pulpit, Priesties, Priest's pintle	Lords and ladies, names associated with the extraordinary cowled spathe.
Parson's nose	Green-winged orchid.
Priest's pintle	Early purple orchid, a venereal herb with strong sexual associations; this name corresponds to the French *testicule de prêtre*. This plant also has holy names such as Gethsemane and Cross flower, its flowers supposed to have been splashed by Christ's blood as he hung on the Cross.
St Candida's eyes	Periwinkle called thus in Dorset (see text).
St John's wort	There are a number of plants named after saints, sometimes because the flowering season is around the time of the saint's feast-day (as is the case with St John's wort, *Hypericum perforatum*).
St Peter's herb, St Peter's keys	Cowslip, from the flowers which resemble a bunch of keys, the badge of St Peter. Legend says that when he dropped the keys, cowslips sprang up from the ground.
Sanctuary	Common centaury, probably a corruption of the *Centaurium* of its scientific name. Also yellow centaury, *Blackstonia perfoliata* and red bartsia.
Star of Bethlehem	Each flower is like a white star, bringing to mind the star which led the three wise men to Bethlehem. Greater stitchwort is also known by this name and as twinkle-star.
Sunday whites	Greater stitchwort in Devon.

Tree of heaven	*Ailanthus altissima*, altissima means very tall which explains the common name.
Trinity flower	Heartsease or wild pansy of which William Bullein wrote 'Three faces in one hodde (hood). . . *herba Trinitatis*'.
Virgin Mary	Used for lungwort and hemp agrimony. Also a prefix in many vernacular names (see 'Lady' names).
Whit Sunday	Wild daffodil, still blooming at this time if Whit is early. Similarly wood sorrel, is a Whitsun flower, and guelder rose is also known as Whitsuntide bosses in the cultivated form. Whitsuntide gilloflower is the double lady's smock in Gloucestershire.
Widow wail, Weeping widow	Snakeshead fritillary, possibly because its flowerheads hang as if in grief and perhaps for the dark colour of the pink ones; dark flowered plants were frequently given 'widow' names.

APPENDIX III

GENERAL BIBLIOGRAPHY

The Church in British Archaeology Morris, Richard (CBA Research Report No 47, London 1983)

Church Poems Betjeman, John, illustrated by John Piper (John Murray, London 1981 Pan Books 1982)

The Churchyards Handbook Stapleton, Revd Henry & Burman, Peter (CIO Publishing, London 1976)

Collins Pocket Guide to English Parish Churches Betjeman, John (ed.) (Collins, London 1968)

English Churchyard Memorials Burgess, Frederick (SPCK, London 1979)

Graves and Graveyards Lindley, Kenneth (Routledge & Kegan Paul, London 1972)

Our Christian Heritage Rodwell, Warwick & Bentley, James (George Philip, London 1984)

FIELD GUIDES

The Birds of Britain and Europe Heinzel, H., Fitter, R., and Parslow, J. (Collins 1974)

Collins Guide to Mushrooms and Toadstools Lange, M. and Hora, B. (Collins 1965)

The Complete Handbook of Garden Plants Wright, Michael (Michael Joseph/Rainbird 1984)

Ferns, Mosses and Lichens of Britain and Northern and Central Europe Jahns, Hans Martin (Collins 1983)

A Field Guide to the Butterflies of Britain and Europe Higgins, L. G. and Riley N. D. (Collins 1975)

A Field Guide to the Insects of Britain and Northern Europe Chinery, Michael (Collins 1973)

A Field Guide to the Reptiles and Amphibians of Britain and Europe Arnold, E. N., Burton K. A. and Ovenden, D. W. (Collins 1978)

Grasses Hubbard, C. E. (Penguin 1968)

The Handbook of Mammals Corbet, G. B. and Southern, H. N. (Blackwell 1977)

Lichens, An Illustrated Guide Dobson, Frank (The Richmond Publishing Co., Orchard Road, Richmond, Surrey, 1981).

The Moths of the British Isles (2 vols) South, Richard (Warne 1961)

The New Field Guide to Fungi Scothill, Eric and Fairhurst, Alan (Michael Joseph 1978)

The Observer's Book of Lichens Alvin, K. L. (and Rose, F.) (Warne 1977)

The Oxford Book of Flowerless Plants Brightman, F. H. (Oxford University Press 1966)

The Oxford Book of Insects Burton, John (Oxford University Press 1973)

The Oxford Book of Invertebrates Nichols, David and Cooke, John (Oxford University Press 1971)

Towns and Gardens Owen, Denis (Hodder & Stoughton 1978)
The Trees of Britain and Northern Europe Mitchell, Alan and Wilkinson, John (Collins 1982)
The Wild Flower Key Rose, Francis (Warne 1981)

APPENDIX IV

WILDLIFE AND CHURCHYARD ORGANIZATIONS

Botanical Society of the British Isles
c/o Department of Botany
British Museum (Natural History)
Cromwell Road
London SW7 5BD

British Butterfly Conservation Society
Tudor House
Quorn
Leicestershire LE12 8AD

British Lichen Society
Conservation Officer:
Dr Anthony Fletcher
Leicestershire Museums Service
96 New Walk
Leicester LE1 6DT

British Trust for Ornithology
Beech Grove
Station Road
Tring
Hertfordshire

Council for the Care of Churches
83 London Wall
London EC2M 5NA
(Information on the legal background to churchyard conservation is available from this source.)

Fauna and Flora Preservation Society
Tony Hutson (Bats)
c/o Zoological Society of London
Regents Park
London NW1 4RY

Mammal Society Bat Group
Phil Richardson
10 Bedford Cottages
Great Brington
Northampton NN7 4JE

Nature Conservancy Council
Northminster House
Peterborough PE1 1UA

Royal Society for Nature Conservation
22, The Green
Nettleham
Lincoln LN2 2NR

Royal Society for the Protection of Birds
The Lodge
Sandy
Bedfordshire SG19 2DL

Other specialist societies which might give advice are:
British Bryological Society (mosses and liverworts)
British Herpetological Society (reptiles and amphibia)
British Mycological Society (fungi)
Conchological Society of Great Britain (molluscs)
Royal Entomological Society (insects)
Addresses of the current secretaries for these societies may be obtained by writing to:
British Museum (Natural History),
Cromwell Road,
London SW7 5BD.

APPENDIX V

THE TWENTY COMMONEST CHURCHYARD BIRDS

The British Trust for Ornithology censused twelve English churches and churchyards during 1971–81, and ranked the commonest breeding birds as follows: blackbird, greenfinch, robin, song thrush, house sparrow, blue tit, wren, dunnock, starling, great tit, chaffinch, goldfinch, spotted flycatcher, linnet, goldcrest, bullfinch, mistle thrush, carrion crow, coal tit, and swift.

187

30 Apr '08

✓

KRZYSZTOF ŻYWCZAK

MADE IN
POLSKA

INTRODUCTION

One contemporary measure of a country's popularity among citizens of the world would be the number of foreign tourists who decide to visit it, and the popularity of goods manufactured in that country in the global market.

WELCOME TO POLAND

Results of a survey conducted by the Polish Tourist Organisation (PTO) concerning the year 2013 confirmed that the satisfaction of foreign tourists visiting Poland remains high. It was estimated at 4.1 on a five-point scale. Citizens of countries with long membership in the European Union are the most willing to recommend visiting Poland to their friends. In their view, Poland is worth visiting because of its beautiful countryside, attractive heritage, delicious cuisine, and relatively low price of services in comparison to Western Europe.

The number of foreigners coming to Poland is steadily increasing. According to data collected and processed by the PTO in 2013, 72 295 000 visitors arrived to Poland that year, of which 15 815 000 were tourists. Among the tourists the dominant group were citizens of the old EU (Germans, British, Dutch, Austrians, Italians, French, and Swedish). Poland hosted 8 020 000 citizens of these countries in that year. Tourists from new EU countries (Czechs, Slovaks, Lithuanians, Latvians and Hungarians) were definitely in the minority and their number amounted to 1 835 000. The number of Ukrainian tourists reached 2 110 000, which was more than the total number of visitors arriving from the new EU countries surveyed. The number of Belarusian tourists was also high and equalled 1 530 000.

Made in Poland

Customers worldwide are increasingly willing to purchase goods with the "Made in Poland" label. In 2013, the value of Polish exports amounted to almost one hundred and fifty-three billion euros, which is the best result ever recorded. In comparison with the result from the previous year, also a record high one, sales increased by 6.5%, including an 11.5% increase in the sale of foodstuffs. The financial effect of this trend is a positive balance of trade in foodstuffs, which, in comparison with 2012, has increased by one-third and amounted to over 5.7 billion euros.

Polish products are bought most willingly in the European Union, which receives two thirds of all Polish exports. Poland's main business partner in Europe is Germany, which has spent over thirty-eight billion euros on Polish products. There is a growing demand for Polish products in the Great Britain, the Czech Republic and countries outside of the European Union, mainly the United States and Norway, as well as Russia, Belarus and Ukraine.

Especially noteworthy is the popularity of Polish foodstuffs, which are in high demand not only in Europe, but also worldwide. They are highly appreciated in the European Union, especially in Germany. The EU receives 78% of food exports from Poland and German consumers spent 4.5 billion euros on Polish food. The second place was taken by the United Kingdom (1.5 billion euros), and third by Russia (1.2 billion euros). Among the leaders terms of the value of Polish food purchased were the Czech Republic, France, Italy, Netherlands, and Slovakia.

"Our top exports are mushroom and rye. Their crops are the highest in the European Union; rye crops are the highest in the world. The second most popular exports are potatoes and apples. Recently, Poland has become the world's leading producer of these crops; in almost every corner of the globe Eve can tempt her Adam with a fruit picked from a Polish tree. Poland also produces significant quantities of sugar beet and is at the forefront (third place) of pig breeding business in the EU. Polish poultry farms are among the largest in the European Union. The country is the fourth largest producer of wheat, oilseed rape, tobacco, and cow's milk. In the years of plenty (most recently in 2010) Polish currant crops accounted for 30% of the global output, and raspberry crops made up 20% of the global output. Polish cheese is increasingly successful in global markets – it accounts for about 3.6% of global output" (Jan Janowski, *Polski eksport 2013 – ponad 150 mld euro!* (*Polish exports in 2013 – more than 150 billion euros!*)).

Top exports

Polish products are sold all over the world, and Polish economy, contrary to what the eternal malcontents stubbornly preach, is becoming more and more innovative, as is illustrated by the numerous examples of excellent Polish products mentioned in this book. Poland's top modern export products, are recognised as symbols of quality in their categories, and their good reputation is projected onto the country in which they were manufactured. There was not enough space in this book to include everything we wanted to cover at greater length, so we have allowed ourselves here to just mention what most deserves to be remembered.

Few countries can threaten Poland's position as a leading manufacturer of furniture, which is exported to one hundred and sixty countries. Up to 90% of furniture made in Poland is sold abroad. Polish factories produce more than thirty million couches, sofas, armchairs, and chairs per year. These products have become its main specialty. It is worth noting that almost half the furniture sold at Ikea was produced in Poland. Polish furniture makers: Black Red White, Nowy Styl, Szynaka Meble, Vox, and Kler are also conquering foreign markets. The latter, which specialises in the production of luxury furniture, caters to the tastes and needs of the world's richest and most powerful people. This is what the owner, Piotr Kler, said about their customers: "Putin bought two furniture sets from us. As we accidentally found out, Leonid Kuchma, the former President of Ukraine, also has Kler furniture – I saw the furniture in pictures from the visit of President Aleksander Kwaśniewski to President Kuchma's summer residence. Initially, we didn't know who it was destined for – orders for the head of the state are placed by interior design companies, which do not reveal who their client is."

Our clothing and shoe manufacturers are very successful. Clothes from Reserved, Cropp, House, Mohito and Sinsay brands, which are owned by Gdańsk-based company LPP, can be purchased in numerous showrooms (over one thousand three hundred)

in twelve countries of Central and Eastern Europe. Shoes from CCC, Boti and Lasocki, which are brands belonging to Poland's largest group of shoe manufacturers, CCC, are worn by people in Poland, the Czech Republic, Slovakia, Hungary, Austria, Slovenia, Croatia, Turkey, Germany, Latvia, Romania, Ukraine and Kazakhstan. More than seven hundred stores of the company are located in these countries. Shoe brands Wojas, Gino Rossi, Bartek, and Gucio are also doing well. Famous people like as Gwyneth Paltrow, Angelina Jolie, and Brad Pitt buy Gucio shoes for their chidren.

Polish cosmetics have an excellent reputation. Colourful eyeshadows, blushers, powders, lipsticks, concealers and eyebrow products by Przemyśl-based manufacturer Inglot are bought by women in more than fifty countries on six continents. Inglot has about four hundred and fifty stores, including a huge showroom in New York. Other producers are also highly successful. Ziaja, based in Gdańsk, has a portfolio of nine hundred cosmetics and pharmaceuticals, and sells its products all over the world, in countries like the Czech Republic, Lithuania, the Philippines, Chile, Japan, South Korea, Taiwan, and Vietnam. Sopot-based Oceanic, the owner of several brands of hypoallergenic cosmetics offered in the AA line, sends its products to nearly thirty countries. Dr Irena Eris enjoys international acclaim in the luxury cosmetics industry.

Huge success was achieved by InPost, which owns the world's largest network of terminals for dispatch and collection of shipments, owning more than three and a half thousand parcel lockers in twenty countries, including Poland and the Czech Republic,

Great Britain, Estonia, Ireland, Lithuania, Latvia, Slovakia, Ukraine, Russia, Saudi Arabia, Chile, Australia, El Salvador, and Guatemala.

One of the most spectacular commercial and branding successes in recent years was achieved by Polish computer game developers. Titles such as *The Witcher*, *Dead Island*, *Painkiller*, *Sniper Ghost Warrior* or *Call for Juarez* are recognised by computer game fans around the world. *The Witcher*, developed by Warsaw-based CD Projekt, occupies a special position in this list. The two editions of the game released so far have sold in seven million copies worldwide. In 2014, an initiative by Prime Minister Donald Tusk, who in 2011 presented Barack Obama with *Witcher 2*, had a curious sequel. During the President of the United States' visit to Poland in June 2014, on the occasion of the twenty-fifth anniversary of the elections on 4 June 1989, Obama referred to the gift he received a few years ago and said: "When I was here last time, Donald gave me a gift; a video game produced in Poland, which has won fans all around the world, called *The Witcher*. I admit that I'm not very good at games, but I know that it's a perfect example of Poland's contribution to the new global economy."

Poland is the world leader in the production of amber jewellery (controlling 70% of the market)

FOLK
HANDICRAFTS

The products of folk artists and craftspeople are very popular among foreign tourists coming to Poland – they serve as original, colourful souvenirs of their visit into the country. Polish people are also developing ineterests in authentic folk art. In the People's Republic of Poland, appreciation of folk art was promoted by the communist regime was the duty of every citizen, which naturally provoked resistance. Artwork in Cepelia-style was regarded as the epitome of artifice and poor taste. Today, regional artists no longer need to subject themselves to central management, and customers willingly buy the objects they produce. In the contest announced in 2009 by Cepelia for new souvenirs from Poland inspired by the folk tradition four hundred and seventy-seven artists submitted eight hundred ninety-four works, which proves that folk art is in renaissance. The artists combined traditional designs and materials with contemporary trends in original and surprising ways. The jury awarded Bogusław Śliwiński's embroidered coasters and the phone pouch made of Koniaków lace by Beata Legierska top places. They also enjoyed the jigsaw puzzles with folk costumes, USB sticks in wooden colourfully painted bird-shaped cases, and flip flops, laptop bags, and gingerbread moulds made with the application of cutout techniques.

Cutouts from Łowicz region

Although various types of cutouts are known in the traditions of various nations (Scandinavia, Germany, Switzerland, Slovakia), nowhere outside Poland have they developed to this extent; nowhere have they been purely folk art, closely related to the cultural panorama of rural life. For this reason, ethnographers regard them as an exclusively Polish art form. Intricate cutouts from Łowicz have for decades been among the most popular souvenirs from Poland. And this is no surprise; their colours and patterns are delightful and they are made with amazing creativity and precision. They were first made in various regions of the country in the middle of the 19th century, when coloured glossy paper appeared on the market. At first they were used to decorate homes

Cutout with a peacock pattern. This type of decoration will enliven apartment walls

and were hung on walls and ceiling beams. They were discovered by painter Leonard Stroynowski, who noticed them during the renovation of the church in Złaków Kościelny near Łowicz; he was fascinated by them immediately, and assembled a substantial collection in a short time, which he then presented in 1901 at an exhibition in Kraków. In order to be considered a cutout a creatively cut paper form must meet one essential criterion: it must be made with coloured glossy paper only. Use of white paper is not allowed.

Cutouts were and are made in many regions of Poland. Well known and appreciated are those created in Kurpie, Sieradz and Lublin regions, and in the areas around Opoczno and Warsaw. However, those made in Łowicz region are the most popular. As the colourful layers are stuck on top of one another, they are sometimes called "stick-ons."

Circular cutout with roosters

TECHNOLOGY

The development of Polish industry, including the automotive industry, after the Second World War started from scratch; there were no factories, technical documentation, or construction and research base, and there were few cooperative industrial facilities. On 6 November 1951, the first Warszawa M-20 rolled out of the Passenger Automobile Factory (FSO) in Żerań. It was made from parts supplied by the Soviet Union. This was the beginning of car production in post-war Poland. According to the latest economic forecasts from 2014, in three years' time, Polish car factories will produce one million cars a year. Currently, the output is not much lower. The lion's share of the production is exported, mainly to Germany, Italy, Great Britain and France. "The quality of cars made in Poland makes them an export hit. This is because all the Polish car factories are perceived within their corporations as being of a very high quality. Some have won the title of best plant within their concerns several times in a row," says Jakub Faryś, President of the Polish Association of the Automotive Industry. Although the origins of the automotive industry in post-war Poland were not easy, the country exported Osa ('Wasp') scooters, as well as cars, an example of which is the Fiat 126p, shortly after starting their production. In Poland, owning a car or motorcycle was often the greatest desire of the average citizen. The heroes of popular series drove *Maluchy*, like Engineer Karwowski in *Czterdziestolatek*, or dreamed of a motorcycle, like Leszek in *Daleko od szosy*. The others had to settle for Romet bicycles, which were also exported under the name Universal.

Passenger Cars

The first Polish car that suited the tastes of customers abroad was the FSO Fiat 125p, which was produced between 1967 and 1991 on an Italian licence and exported to more than eighty countries. Its successor was the Polonez, produced from 1978 to 2002. It had a completely new bodywork designed by Fiat engineers in cooperation with FSO stylists. Its shape was markedly different from the shape of the cars previously produced in Żerań, and its basic version had

The Fiat 125p was the first Polish vehicle to be exported

The Polish Fiat 126p

The Polish Fiat 126p, 1973

five doors. The bonnet, which was sloped forwards, and the steep slope of the windshield, made the car more aerodynamic, and its drag coefficient was about 16% lower than that of the Fiat 125p. The car's standard equipment stood out in its class. It had a movable steering column, which allowed the drivers to adapt its position to their preferences.

Although the teams of engineers, designers and stylists from the Centre for Research and Development of Passenger Cars at FSO presented updated versions of the Polonez each year, the car did not achieve the same measure of success abroad as did the Fiat 125p. Polonezes were exported to forty countries, mainly in Europe, but also to Egypt. In the 1990s, the Polonez was also manufactured in China.

The next model, which proved to be a real hit, was the Fiat 126p, produced in the assembly halls of the Small-Engined Car Factory (FSM) in Bielsko-Biała. The pioneering *Maluch*, assembled entirely from parts supplied by the Fiat factory in Cassino, left the Bielsko factory on 6 June 1973. This date should be regarded as the beginning of the Polish automotive revolution, as a result of which cars became available to the people. Although the communist government declared that the car would be widely available to the average person, the reality of purchasing it bordered on the miraculous. It cost quite a lot, as its price was the equivalent of twenty times the value of contemporary average monthly salary, and, in addition to that, most of the output was exported to Italy under a licence agreement. Production of the Fiat 126p ended twenty-seven years later, in September 2000. In Poland, 3 318 674 of these vehicles were made. The *Maluch* was exported to many European countries, as well as Cuba and China, where it found use as taxis, Chile, New Zealand, Egypt, and Australia. Due to the simple structure and low operating costs, they were popular in developing countries such as Sri Lanka, Bangladesh, Zaire, and India.

Few people know that other Polish cars were quite popular in foreign countries. As Andrzej Krajewski wrote: "Żuk vans, which were produced in Lublin, conquered Egypt and Colombia. On the Nile, these vans were even transformed into fire engines and buses. The Egyptian government purchased a licence and, under the name Ramses, the Żuk was produced in a factory near Cairo until 1998."

The Polonez was designed by Fiat engineers in cooperation with FSO stylists

Polonez – with big bumpers and plastic bars complementing the modern profile

PLACES

There is no shortage of attractive and beautiful places in Poland. According to a survey conducted by the Polish Tourist Organisation in the second half of 2013, foreign tourists primarily associate our country with a visit to city landmarks and museums, forests, national parks, sites on the UNESCO World Heritage List, mountains, lakes, cultural events, hiking, winter sports, and the beaches of the Baltic Sea. Among the places they would wish to visit when returning to Poland, they mentioned cities, sites on the UNESCO World Heritage List, and national parks and forests. To some extent, the results of the PTO survey coincide with the findings of the report prepared by Simon Anholt, an expert on issues related to country branding. As was stated in an article discussing this report, published by *Polityka* weekly, "Foreign tourists, rather than the Baltic (which is not the warmest of seas) or the Tatras (which are not the highest or most extensive mountains), prefer to visit the Białowieża Primeval Forest and the Bieszczady Mountains. This is another paradox: what we associate with backwardness, to them is the last patch of untouched nature in Europe." Although the strategies of institutions involved in promoting Poland abroad vary, these are places that, regardless of periodic trends and fashions, are invariably popular among Polish people and visitors arriving from all over the world.

Kraków

For a number of years, Kraków has maintained the top position in rankings of places enjoying the greatest popularity among foreign tourists visiting Poland. It is the most recognisable city among foreigners, who, above all, appreciate its magical atmosphere, created by its increasingly beautiful heritage sites, formidable in their age and importance, as well as the quiet, intimate corners where historical reserve disappears, replaced by liberty and relaxation. Kraków's success probably stems from the fact that for centuries it has followed its own rhythm, lived by its own rules, paying no attention to the momentary and transient fashions and novelties which appear in the world. In 2013, the capital of Małopolska was visited by 9.2 million tourists, of which 2.5 million were visitors from abroad. This group has increased by two hundred thousand since 2012. The most numerous were the British and Germans, as well as the Spanish and Italians. The numbers of visitors from Russia, Hungary, the Czech Republic, and the Netherlands increase every year.

Confirmation of Kraków's dominant position is provided by the rankings prepared by specialist online travel websites like TripAdvisor, as well as traditional media. Kraków took fifteenth place in the ranking of the world's most beautiful cities prepared by the prestigious American magazine *Condé Nast Traveller*, published in November 2013. Eighty thousand readers who had succumbed to the charm of the architecture and the old Polish tradition were involved in the preparation of the list of twenty-five of the world's greatest cities. Their appraisal was the sum of the cultural value and of purely practical aspects of travel, which is evidenced by the fact that the final opinion was also influenced by factors such as friendliness towards tourists, and accommodation and catering facilities. It is worth noting that Kraków obtained the same score as Prague, and was ahead of such famous resorts as Seville, Paris, Venice, and Barcelona.

Foreign tourists visiting Kraków especially appreciate the excellent conditions for relaxing and beautiful sites, among which the most popular are the Old Town, especially the Main Market Square, the Royal Route, Wawel Castle and Kazimierz. More and more people who come to Kazimierz go also to Podgórze to discover the fascinating modern historical museum located

The Cloth Hall has served as a place of trade for Kraków's stallholders for centuries

The bugle call played every day from the tower of St. Mary's Basilica is a big attraction

Wawel Hill is situated in the historical
district of Kraków

Today the Cloth Hall hosts two rows of stalls, as well as the famous Noworolski Café. The upper floor houses the Gallery of 19th-Century Polish Art

in the former Schindler factory and the MOCAK Museum of Contemporary Art. It is worth noting that Kraków's museums are also appreciated by the editors of CNN. In 2014, the Polish Aviation Museum was in the top ten of the list of the fourteen best aviation museums in the world developed by them. This Kraków museum, founded in 1963, has since 2010 been housed in a new, impressive building that from a bird's eye view resembles a spinning propeller. This building, as well as several other ones, such as the now classic Manggha Museum of Japanese Art and Technology or the Kraków Arena, opened in 2014, which is a new sports and event venue second to none in Poland and worldwide – mean that the former capital of Poland can be associated not only with a fascinating history, but with modernity as well. Also highly popular is exploring the Rynek Underground, which was opened to tourists in September 2010. In this unique museum, which is in

The façade and gate of the church of Sts. Peter and Paul in Kraków

The monument of the legendary Wawel Dragon
near the Dragon's Den cave

A Jewish cemetery in Kraków

music concerts performed by the best orchestras in the world, and three festivals: Seven Traditions, Crossroads, and Beethoven Festival. In 2016, the title of the European Capital of Culture will be awarded to another Polish city; Wrocław, which defeated Białystok, Bydgoszcz, Gdańsk, Katowice, Lublin, Łódź, Poznań, Toruń, Szczecin, and Warsaw.

Tourists visiting Kraków do not limit themselves to staying in the city, but also explore the surrounding areas. Many visit Wadowice, the hometown of Pope St. John Paul II, where a modern multimedia museum dedicated to the Polish Pope was opened in 2014, and the sanctuary at Kalwaria Zebrzydowska.

fact an archaeological reserve, the history of the city and its relationships with Europe are presented in a state-of-the-art manner.

Many people are curious about the story of the Wawel dragon, and a visit to its caves is especially enjoyed by children. Both children and adults cannot pull themselves away from the stalls with regional souvenirs and folk handicrafts in the Cloth Hall.

A tribute to the strength of Kraków's European cultural tradition, as well as its contemporary aspirations, was the honour of being awarded the title of European City of Culture by the European Union in the jubilee year 2000 – four years before Poland's accession to the European Union. Along with eight other cities, for twelve months Kraków became one of the European centres of cultural life. More than five hundred and seventy events were organised then, among which the most popular and acclaimed were series of classical

A romantic lane in the Jewish district
of Kazimierz in Kraków

Wieliczka

One of the top tourism sites in Małopolska is the Wieliczka Salt Mine – one of the main attractions of the region, added to the UNESCO World Natural and Cultural Heritage List in 1978. Visiting it is a real journey into the depths of the Earth. To descend the depth of one hundred thirty five metres under ground, one must go down eight hundred steps. Fortunately, a mining lift can also be used to return to the surface. Three kilometres of underground corridors and more than twenty chambers, in which everything, including the most minute details, is made of salt, are available for exploration. The parts which visitors admire the most are the Chapel of St. Kinga and the light show on the shores of a saline lake. According to legend, the mine in Wieliczka was established thanks to Kinga, who, when leaving her Hungarian home and setting off to Poland, dropped a ring into one of the Hungarian salt shafts and rediscovered it in a rock of salt dug out near Kraków. After visiting the mine, you can eat in an underground tavern where no guest has ever complained that the dishes are unsalted. All these

The Weimar Chamber

**The Weimar Chamber was named after the birthplace
of the German poet Johann Wolfgang von Goethe.
He was one of the mine's first guests**

The Chapel of St. Kinga. It hosts Masses in honour of the patron St. Kinga and St. Barbara, and midnight Masses

attractions are waiting on the most popular tourist route, which has been taken by more than thirty six million people from around the world. It is worth knowing that the area accessible to tourists is only a small portion of the mine, which has about three hundred kilometres of corridors and three thousand chambers. The depth of the mine is three hundred twenty seven metres, and therefore it could hold Poland's tallest building – Warsaw's Palace of Culture and Science – with room to spare.

It is worth knowing that the tradition of salt mining in Wieliczka dates back six thousand years. In no other place in Europe have archaeologists discovered older traces of saltworks. Contemporary inhabitants of these areas obtained salt by evaporating brine flowing from saltwater springs. The contemporary history of the mine dates back to the 12th century, when more efficient methods of brine evaporation were developed. The breakthrough came in the 13th century. It was then that countless layers of rock salt were discovered.

The Russegger IV Chamber. It holds vertical transportation equipment, including a treadmill (extraction machine)

The salt figure of St. Kinga

Bochnia

The salt mine in Bochnia, which became a UNESCO World Heritage Site in 2013 also abounds in attractions. Mining began here in the first half of the 13th century, and the depth of three hundred metres was reached by the 15th century. A record depth of four hundred and seventy metres was reached in the second half of the 20th century. One curious fact is that until the end of the 1990s the Campi shaft used a steam engine. It was the longest operating device of its type in Poland. The mine in Bochnia is a venerable record holder, which prides itself on the title of the oldest mine in Poland. Today, the place of miners has been taken by tourists.

Since the Underground Multimedia Exposition was opened in Bochnia in 2011, visiting the mine is a journey in time, and a new, extraordinary life is emerging in the salt corridors and chambers. The journey back in time begins in the age of Bolesław the Shy and Kinga, and the colourful, historic walk is enlivened by characters associated with the history of the mine, interactive

Antique steam engine – Campi Shaft

The Chapel of St. Kinga

Ważyn Chamber – educational visits for children

Mysiur Chamber – until the 1960s it was a stable for horses that had been used to transport heavy lumps of salt at the turn of the 16th century. The use of animals was only abandoned in the 1960s, when electricity was first used in the mine. The attraction of the brine-flooded Chamber 81 is an unforgettable boat trip. Unusually impressive is the vast Ważyn chamber. It is 255 metres long, 14.5 meters wide, more than seven metres high, and is located 50 metres under ground. A visit to the underground world of the mine in Bochnia is also an opportunity to try the 140m-long slide, which was built in the former ramp connecting the Ważyn Chamber to the August Level. Those who prefer to move between levels in a more traditional way can use the stairs built next to it. Another unforgettable experience is the journey on the underground railway. About one hundred and fifty thousand Polish and foreign tourists visit the mine in Bochnia every year.

presentations, models illustrating the development of mining technology, and videos displayed on special screens. The tour leads visitors through the 18th-century

ŁÓDŹ

Łódź boasts one of the most original art galleries in Poland – Urban Forms. Its uniqueness lies mainly in the fact that the space, in which the works by international artists are presented, is the city itself, and more specifically, the walls in the city, which are decorated with unusual and fabulously colourful large format paintings by street artists. Among the dozens of works is one in particular that was made in autumn 2013 on the side wall of a ten-storey block at 80 Wyszyńskiego Boulevard and is the largest mural in Poland. The artist is a Chilean nicknamed Inti. The Chilean painted the mural whilst standing in the bucket of a large crane which lifted him to a height of

**The mural at 19 Legionów Street
by Polish artist M-City**

several dozen metres. His activities were followed every day with curiosity by the residents of Łódź and of other cities. Among the artists who were invited to paint on the walls of Łódź townhouses are such famous street artists as the Brazilian duo Os Gêmeos and the promising Aryz

**Etam Crew – a group of Polish artists –
created the mural at 3 Uniwersytecka Street**

from Spain. Os Gêmeos have painted in New York, São Paulo, Buenos Aires, Lisbon, Berlin, and also in London, where they changed the face of the entrance to one of the world's most famous galleries – the Tate Modern. The wall in Łódź at 27 Kościuszki Boulevard was decorated by the Etam Crew (Poland) and Sat One (Germany). The mural on the corner of Pomorska and Kilińskiego Streets is the work of the Spaniard El Kenora, and the one on the corner of Zachodnia and Próchnika Streets – by Remeda from France. Among Polish artists were M-City, Otecki, Lump Michał "Sepe" Wręga, Daniel "Chazme" Kalinowski, and Etan Crew, which is Przemysław "Sainer" Blejzyk and Mateusz "Bezt" Gapski. The murals sparkle with vivid colours, surprising ideas and execution, and the variety means that art lovers following their trail through the grey city are eager to be surprised by the next work.

The gallery was established in 2009 as an initiative by the Urban Forms Foundation. People involved in initiating and implementing it have plans to extend the gallery with other urban art objects, such as sculptures and installations. The gallery has become a highlight attracting art lovers from around the world to Łódź. They can participate in tours and workshops organised by the Foundation, buy merchandise from the online store (t-shirts, folders, bags, mugs, postcards), and participate in the urban art festival organised every year in the autumn.

Chilean artist Inti made the mural at 80 Wyszyńskiego Boulevard, block 267 (Retkinia Estate)

The mural at 12 Uniwersytecka Street by Polish artist Sainer

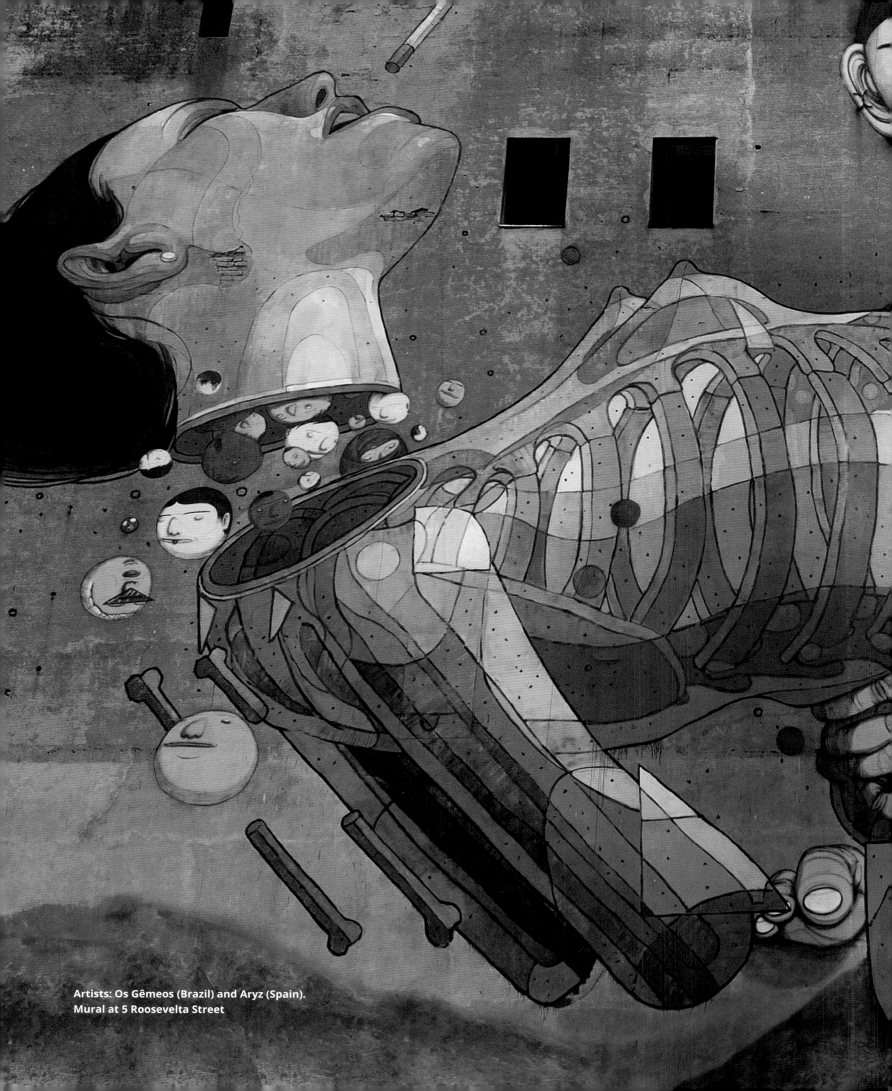

Artists: Os Gêmeos (Brazil) and Aryz (Spain).
Mural at 5 Roosevelta Street

Masuria

In November 2011, the Swiss foundation New7Wonders announced the list of winners of a competition for seven new natural wonders of the world. Although Masuria, which took part in the competition, was not in the top seven, the place it took – in the top 14 of the 28 finalists – was a great success, as the Polish representative overtook all its European rivals as well as such famous world sites as the Grand Canyon in Colorado, the Maldives, and the Galapagos Islands. How did Masuria's adventure with the competition start? In 2007, the Swiss foundation New7Wonders announced a competition for seven new wonders of nature. The Polish Tourist Organisation proposed three candidates: the Great Masurian Lakes, the Białowieża Primeval Forest, and the Błędów Desert. After multi-stage qualification, Masuria was the only candidate representing Poland, and it eventually reached the final round. The fact that victory in the competition is not just a matter of prestige is evidenced by the example of the earlier New7Wonders Foundation contest for seven new architectural wonders of the world. Some of the buildings that triumphed; for example Machu Picchu, the Taj Mahal, and Petra, recorded a significant increase in interest from tourists and an increasing number of visitors: Machu Picchu by a fifth, the Taj Mahal by one-third, and Petra by nearly seventy percent.

The Masuria promotional campaign, organised under the slogan "Masuria – The Wonder of Nature", was supported by the Ministries of Sport and Tourism, Foreign Affairs, and National Education, branch organisations of the Polish Tourist Organisation and the Polish Chamber of Tourism, Presidents Bronisław Komorowski, Aleksander Kwaśniewski, and Lech Wałęsa, Cardinal Stanisław Dziwisz, as well as Andrzej Wajda and Mirosław Hermaszewski. The promotional campaign emphasised those characteristics that might gain international recognition in the eyes of the jury: the picturesque post-glacial landscape with lakes and lakelets shimmering among green forests, the cultural heritage of the many generations of people inhabiting the region, and also the perfect conditions for sports, especially sailing and kayaking, but also fishing and diving, hiking, cycling, and horse riding.

View of Lake Wigry